Birds - A Coloring Book
for Adults and Teens

A Collection of 40 Colorful Birds From Around the World

We hope you enjoy coloring these colorful birds
and bringing them to life!

For more information about other books available by
DB Atkins visit

www.dbacolor.com

Produced by ATC, LLC
ISBN: 979-8394121029

Coloring Tips

Using Crayons?

Keep your crayons sharp for fine details. You can use a toothpick to add fine detail into the wax after its been put on the page.

Using Colored Pencils?

Start with an even base color by using the side of the pencil. Then come back and use varying pressure to add shadows or highlights on top of the base color.

Using Watercolor Paint?

Start with the lightest color you plan on using, adding darker colors as you progress. Don't forget to blot your brush on a paper towel befoer touching the brush to a page to prevent the color from spreading in a way you dont want.

To AX & HE with love

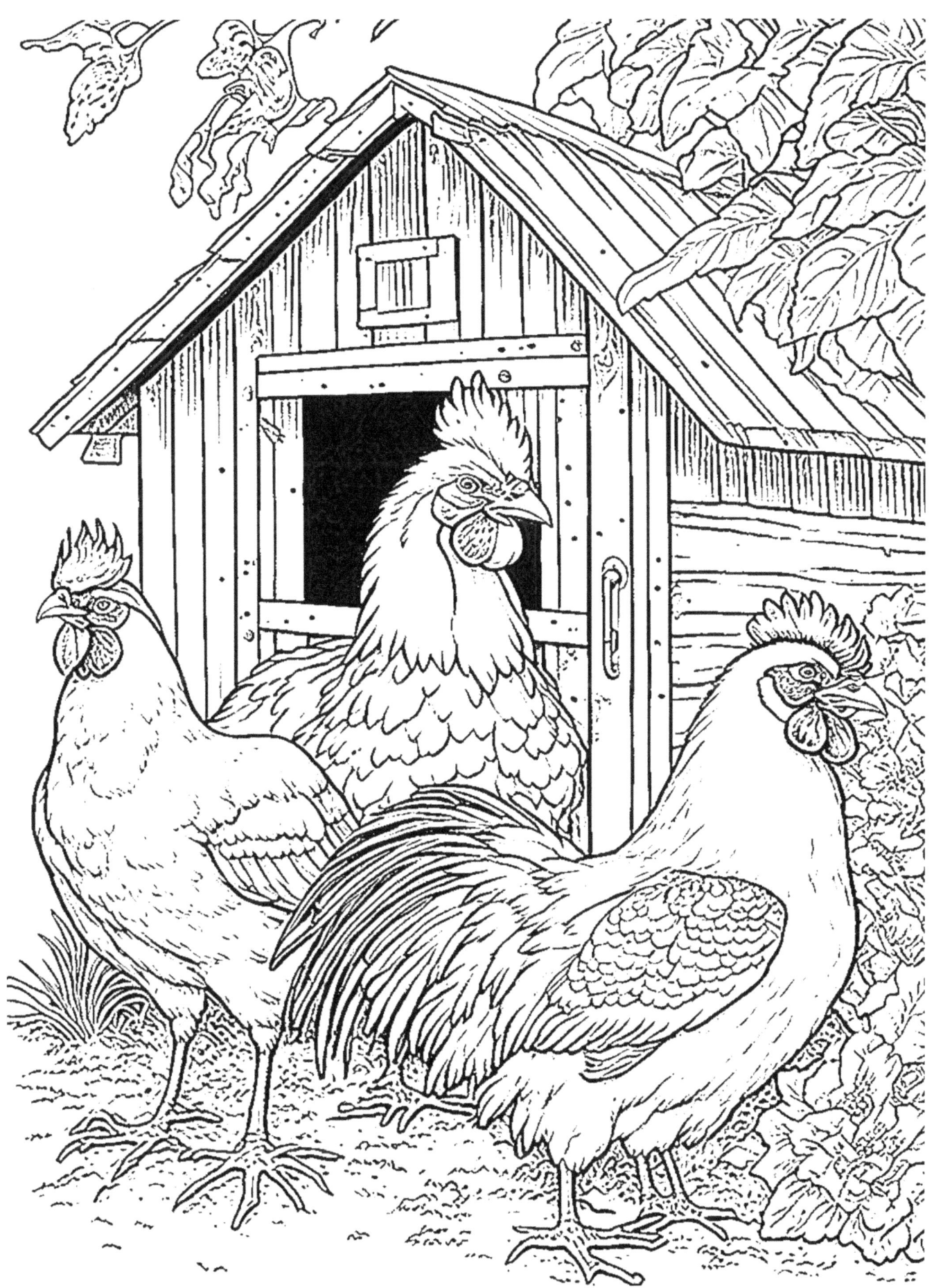

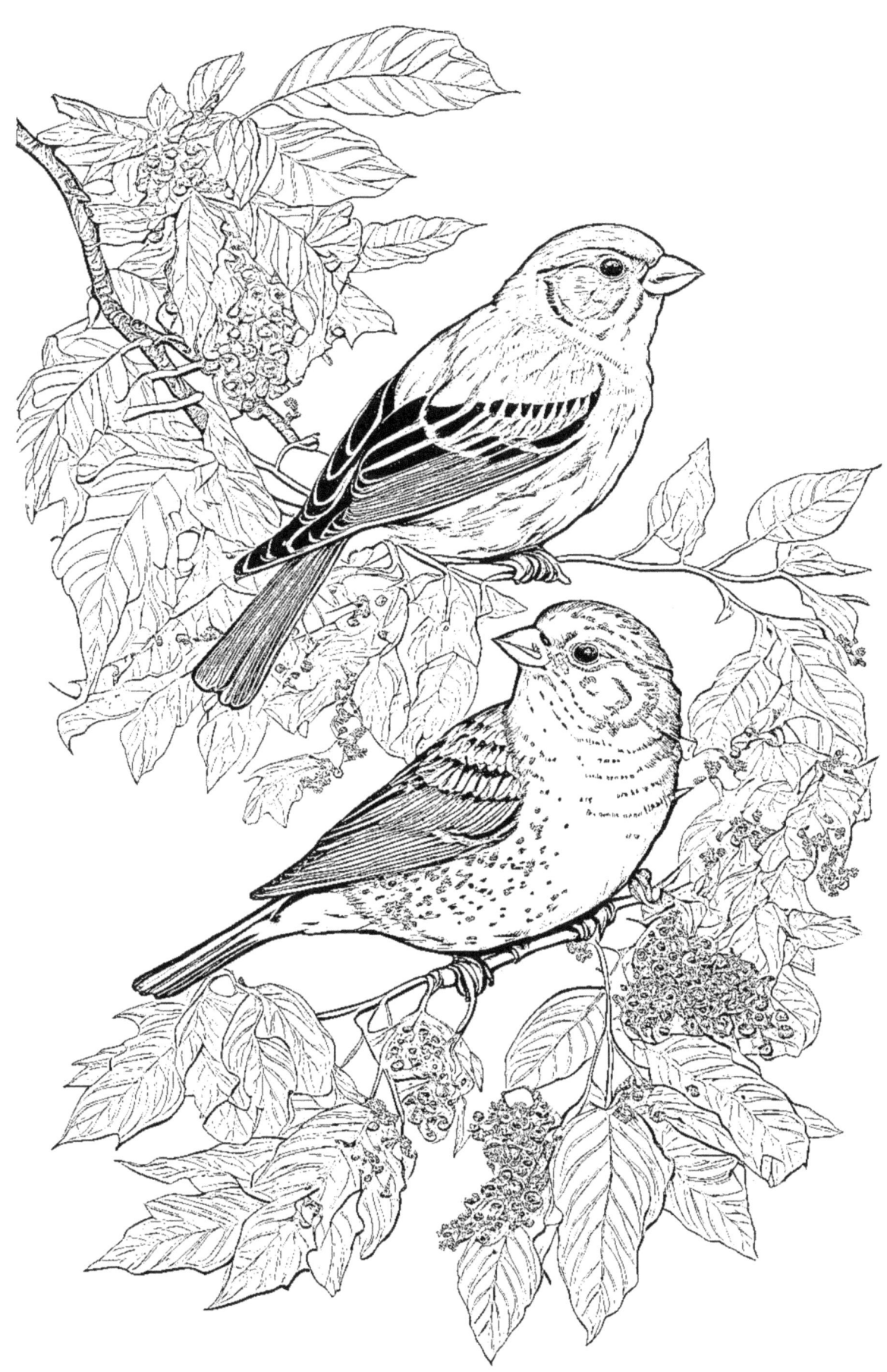

2 - Gold Finches

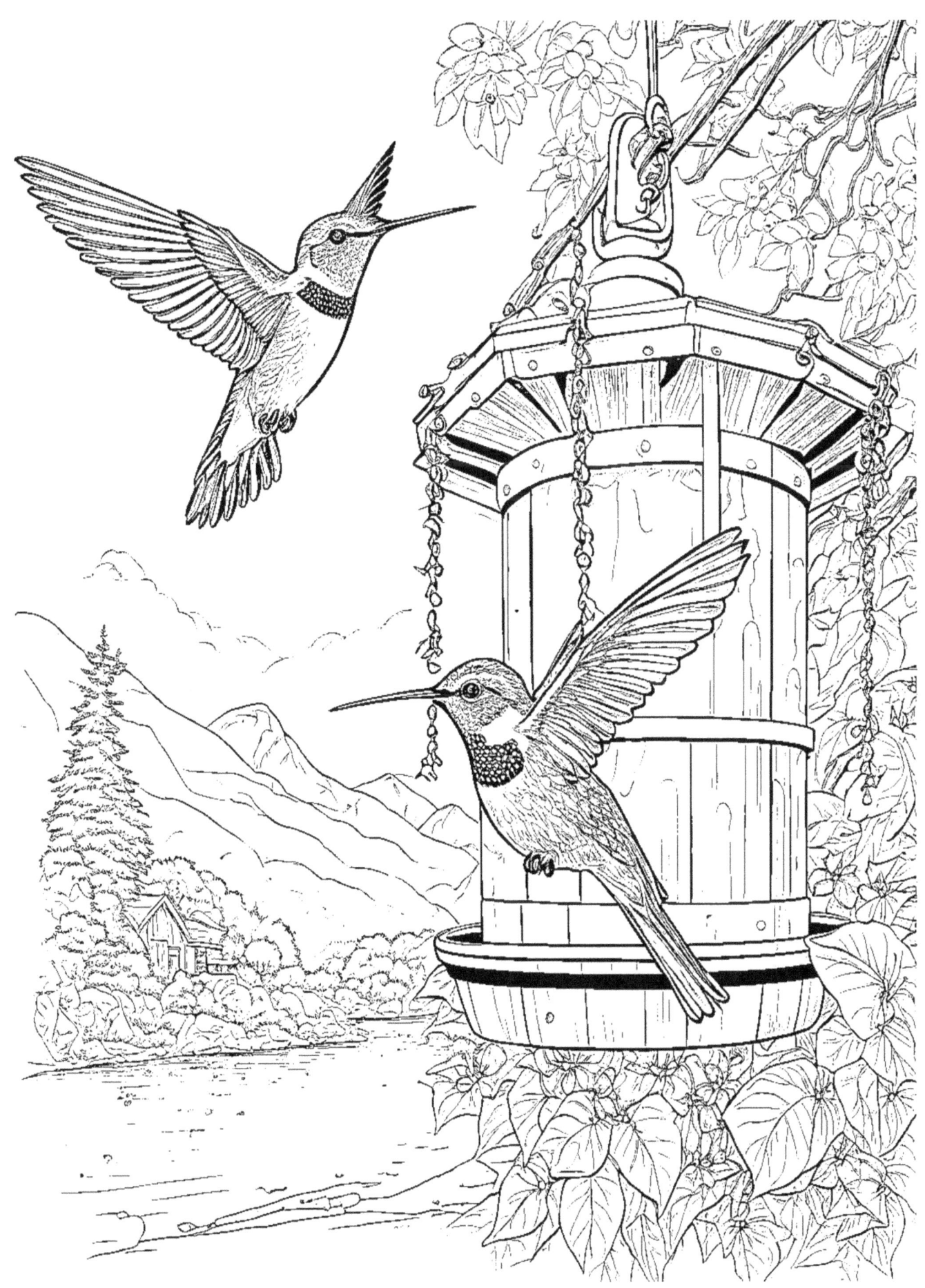

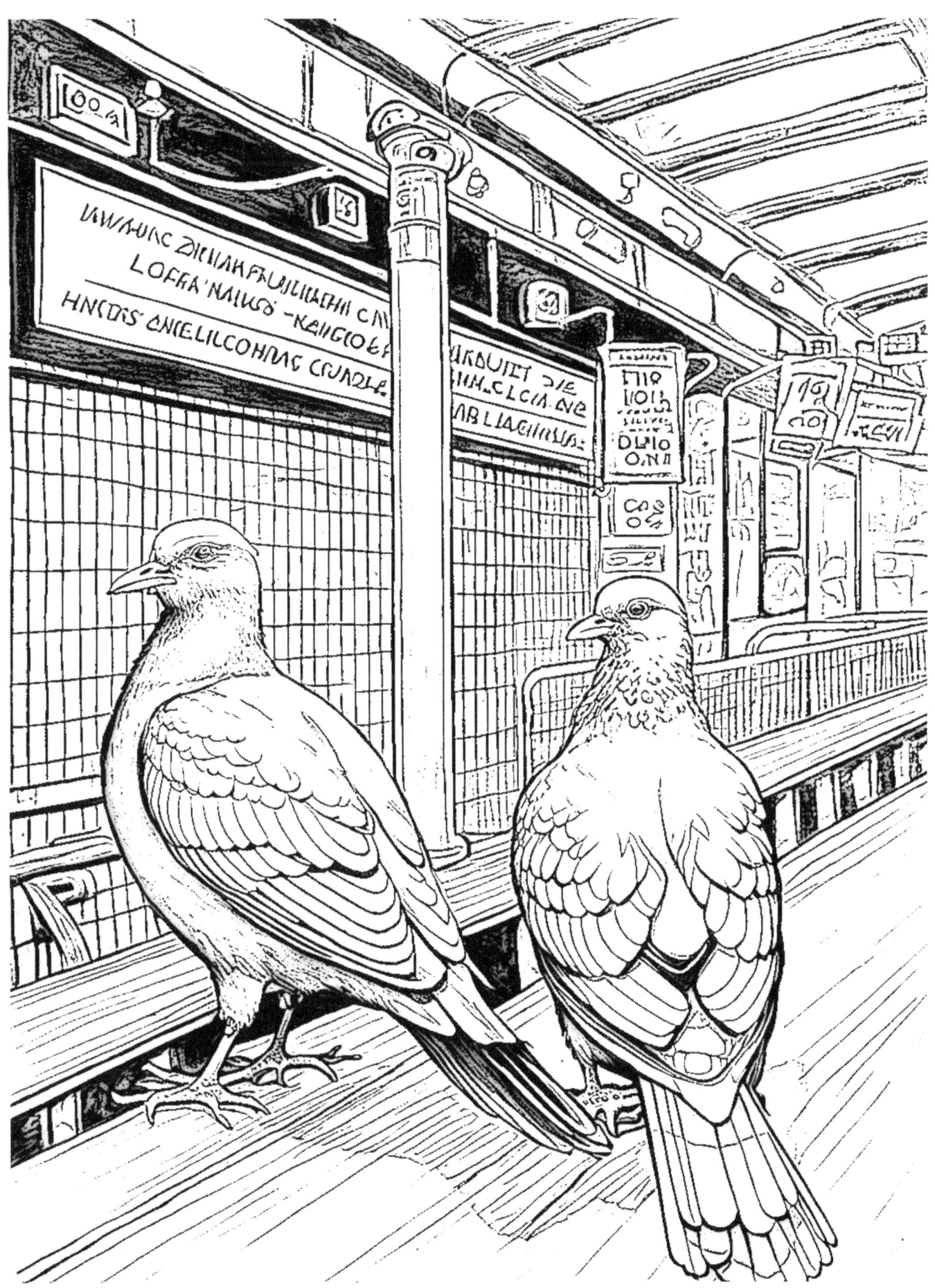

4 - Pigeons

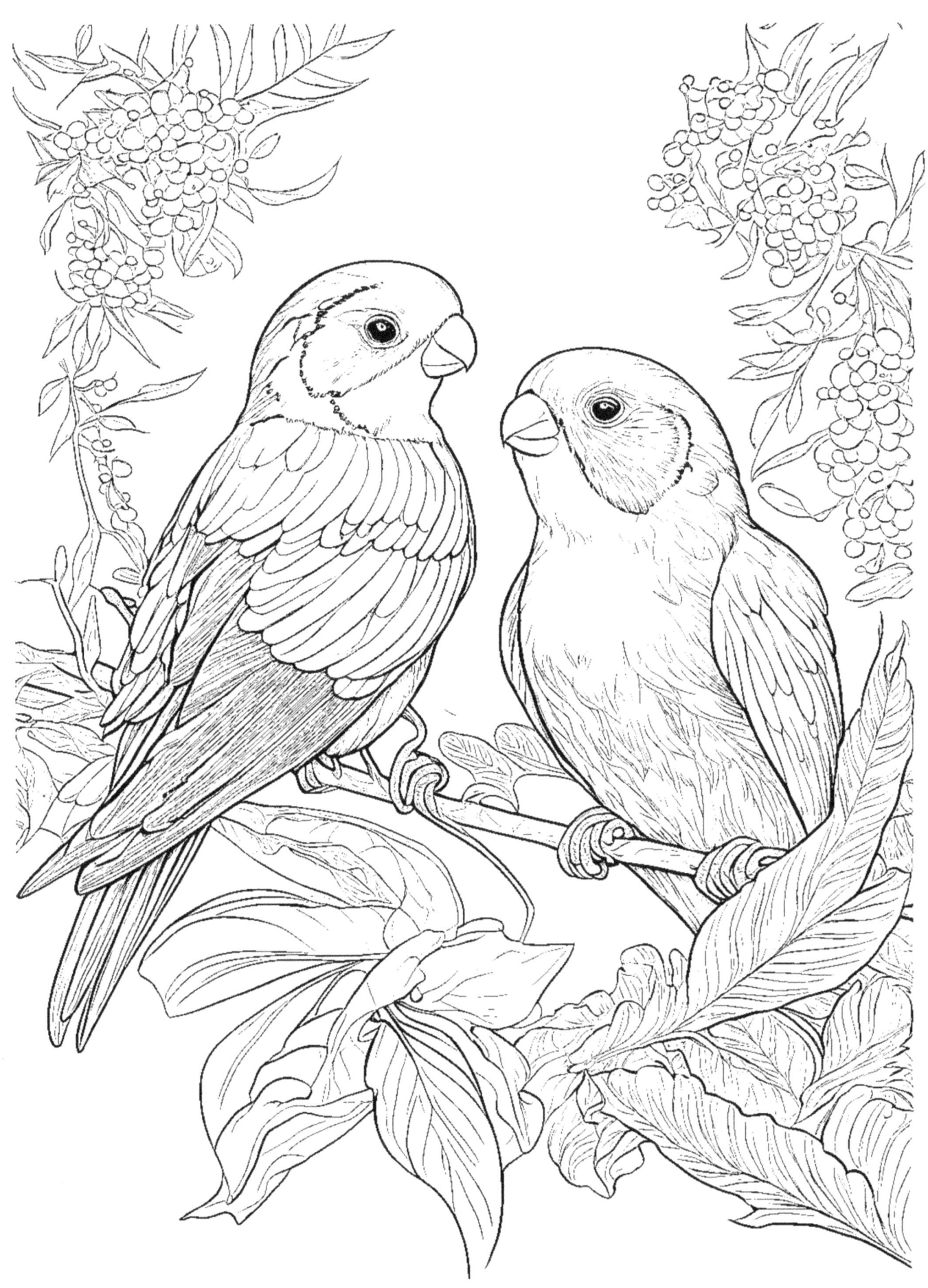

5 - Yellow Collard Lovebirds

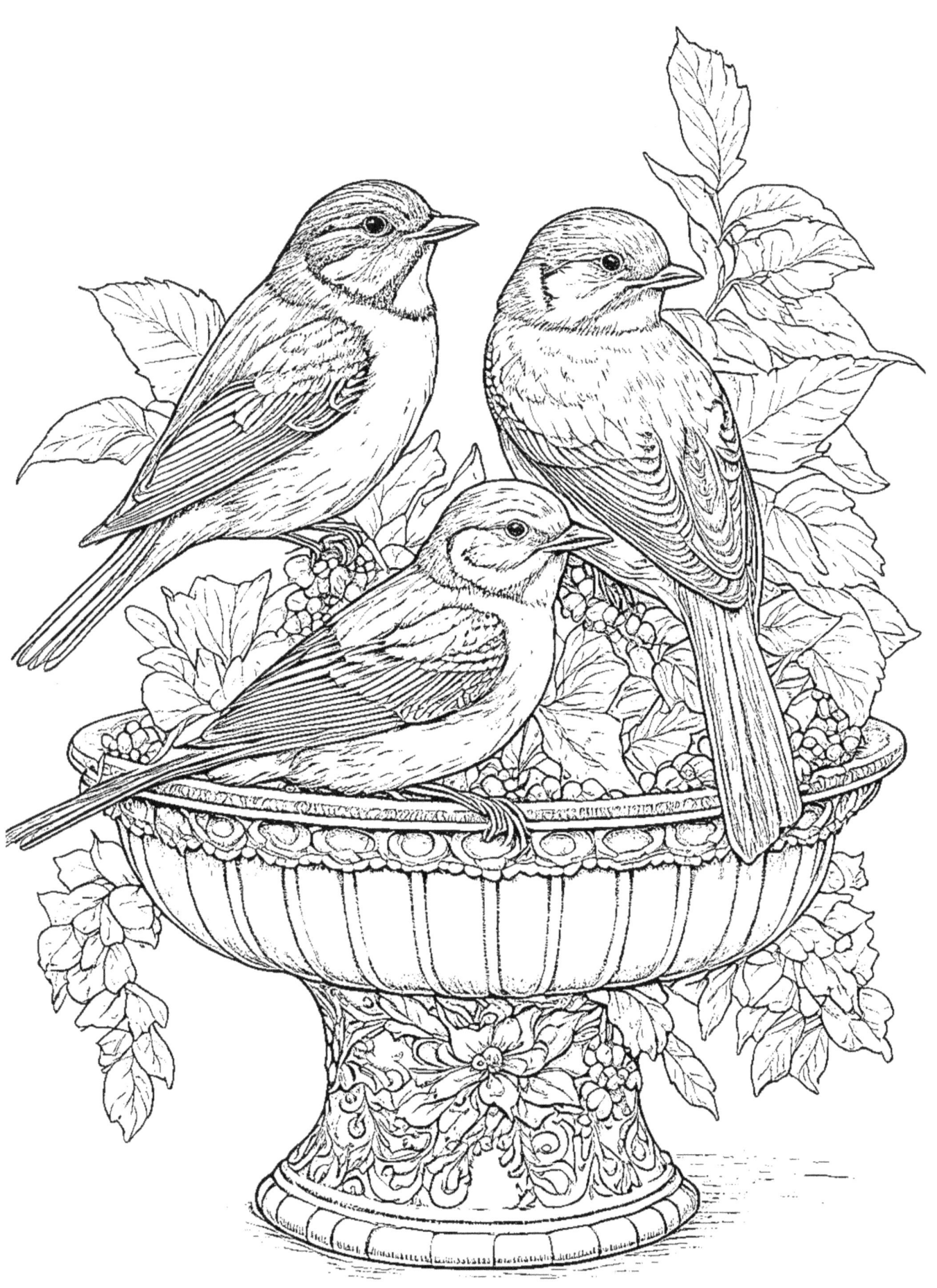

6 - Bluebirds

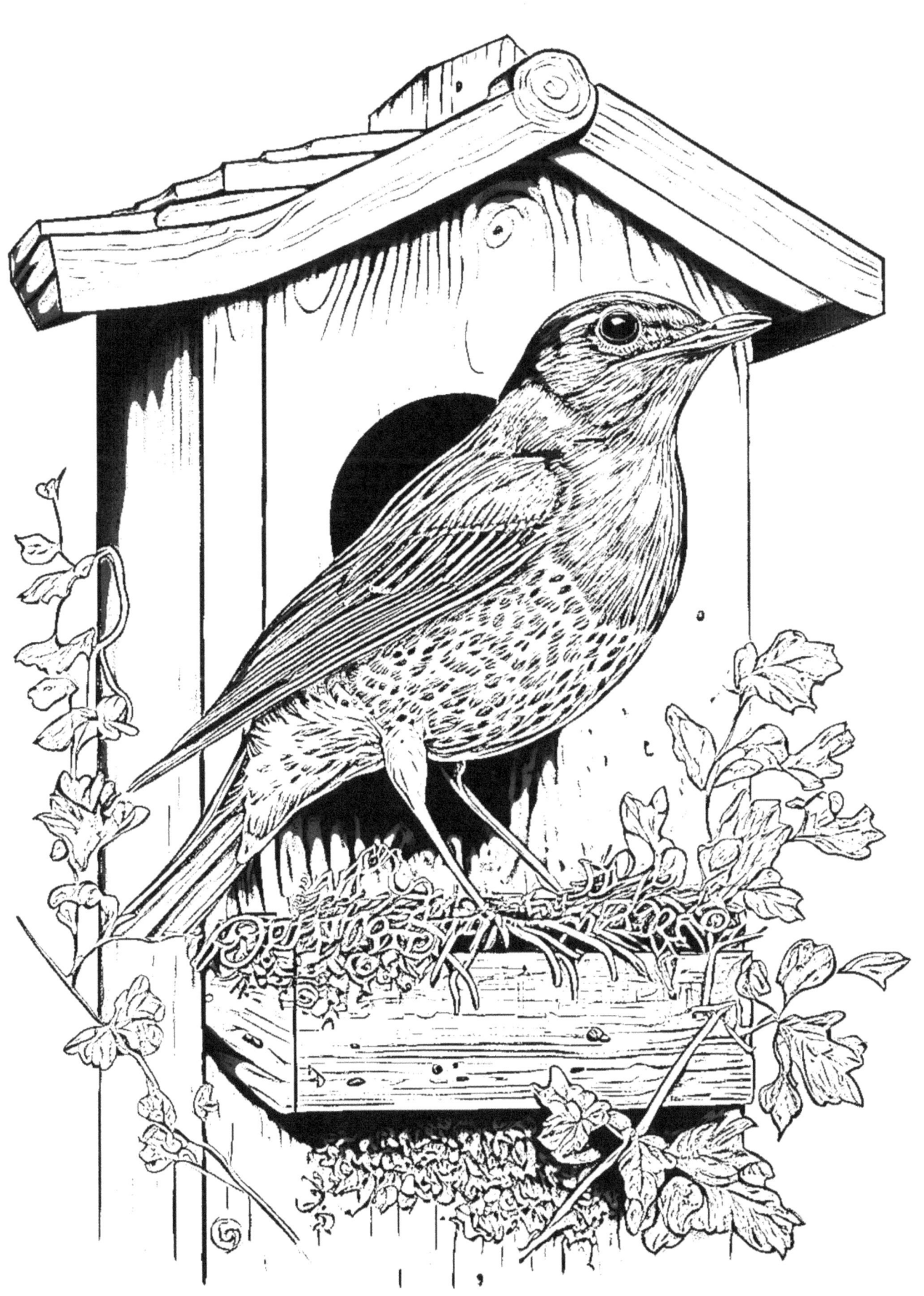

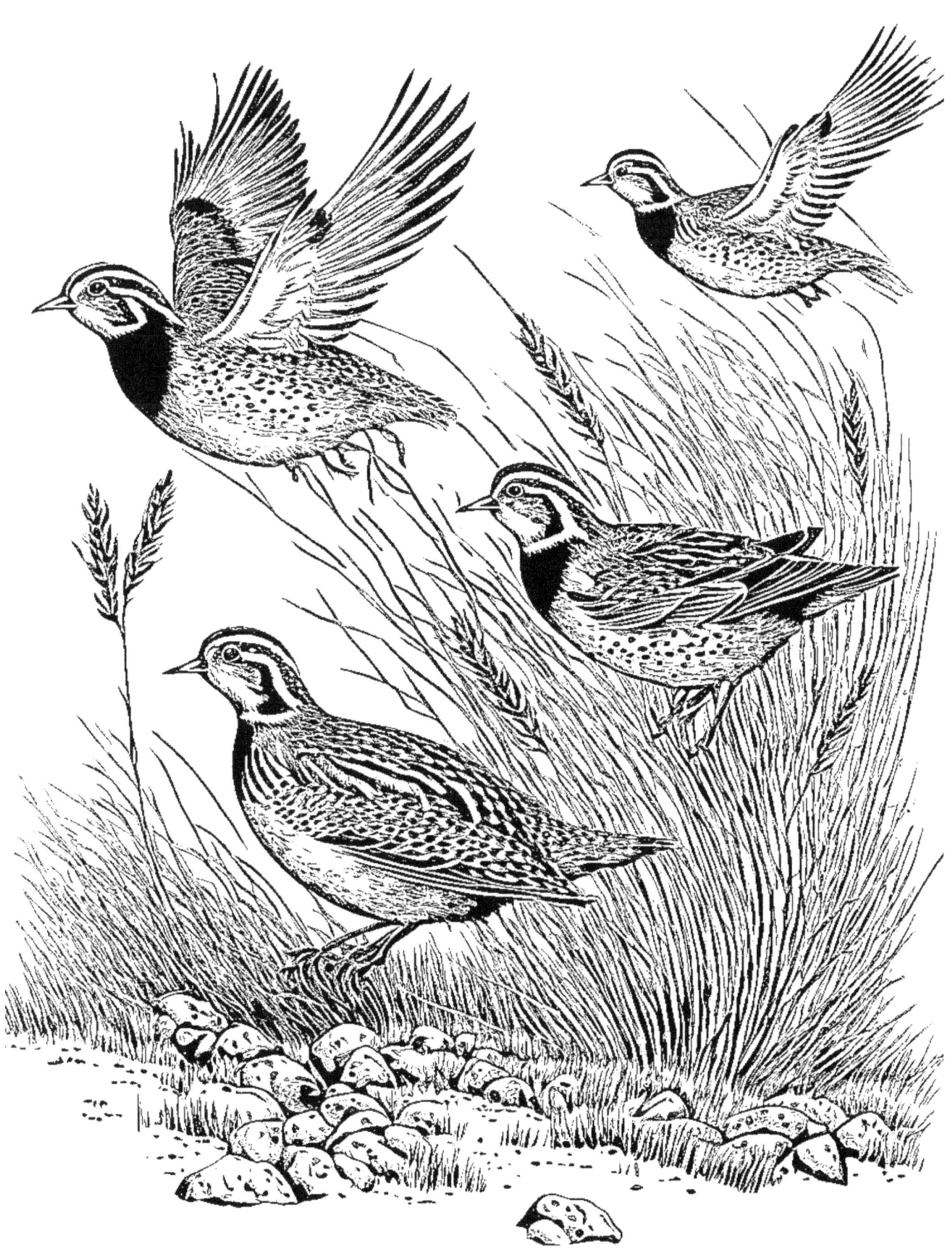

8 - Quail

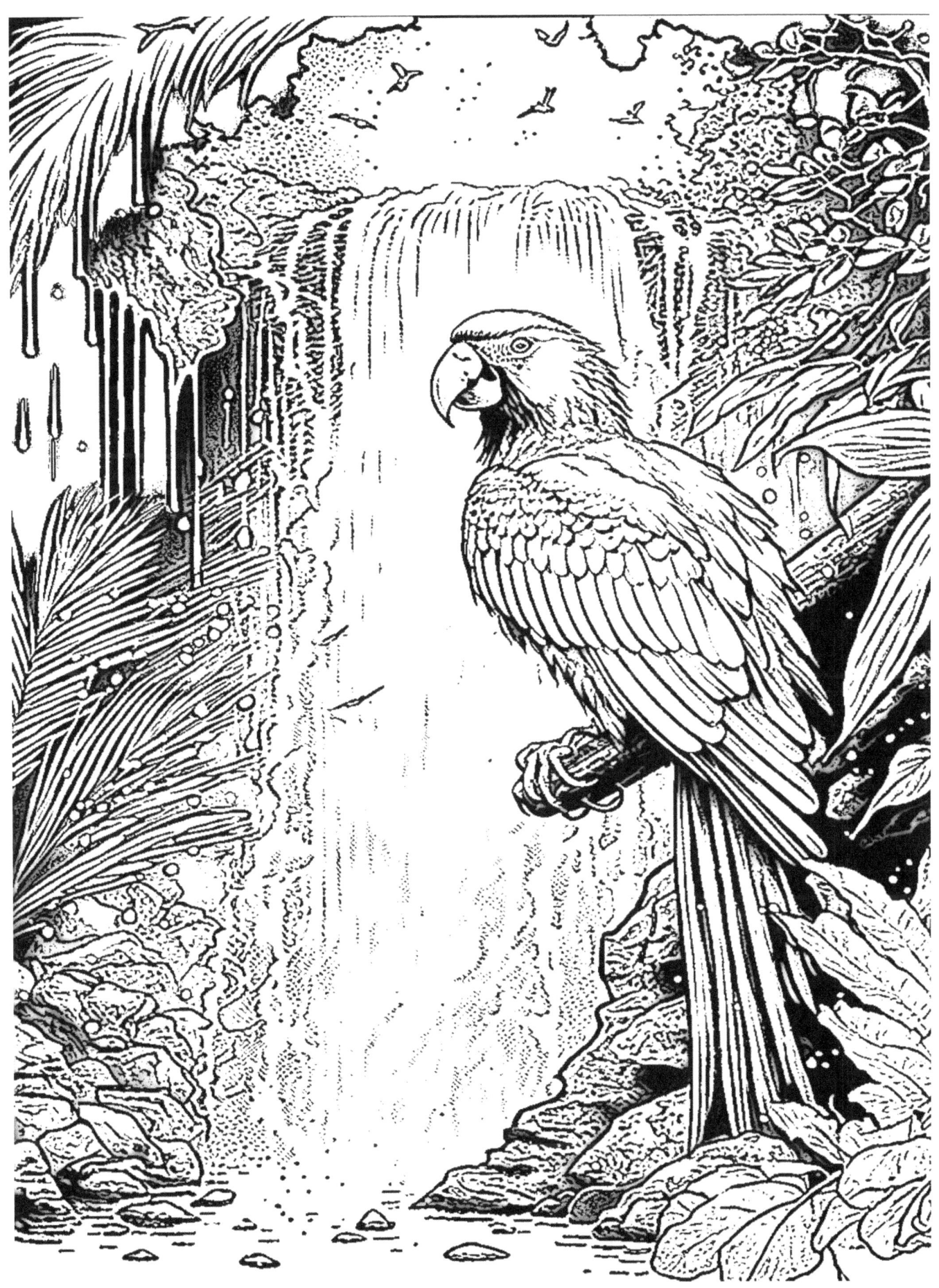

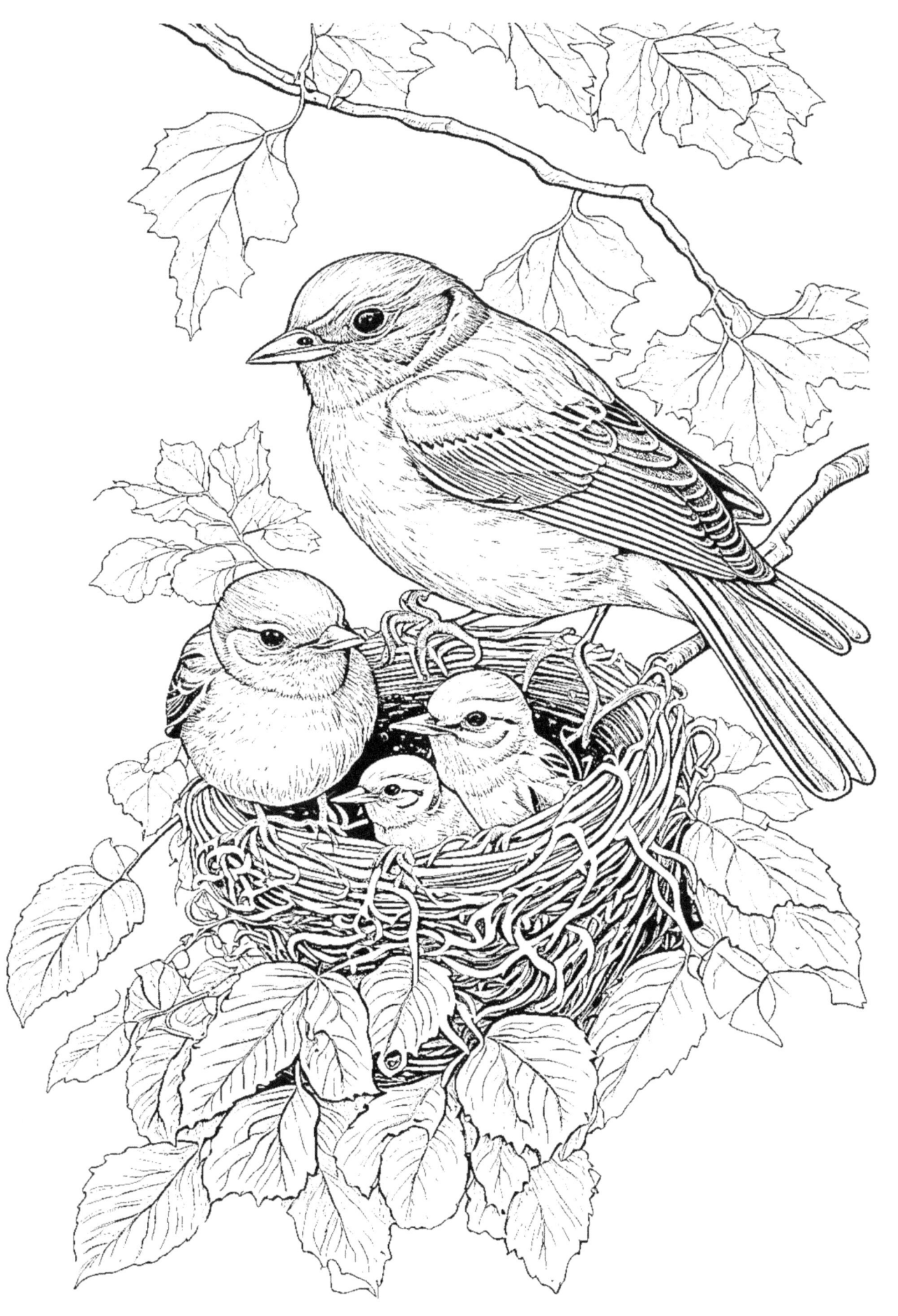

10 - Bluebirds in Nest

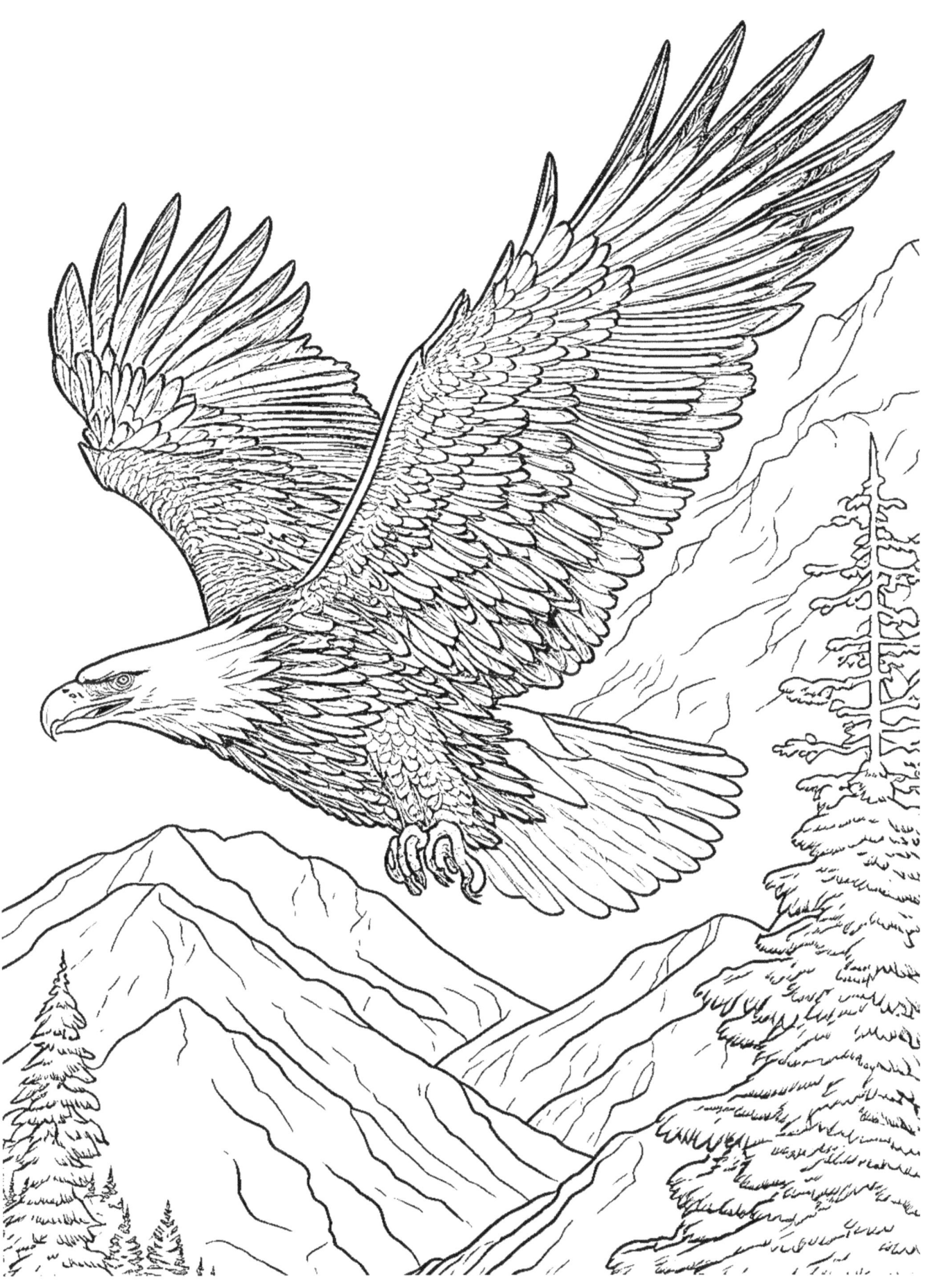

11 - Bald Eagle

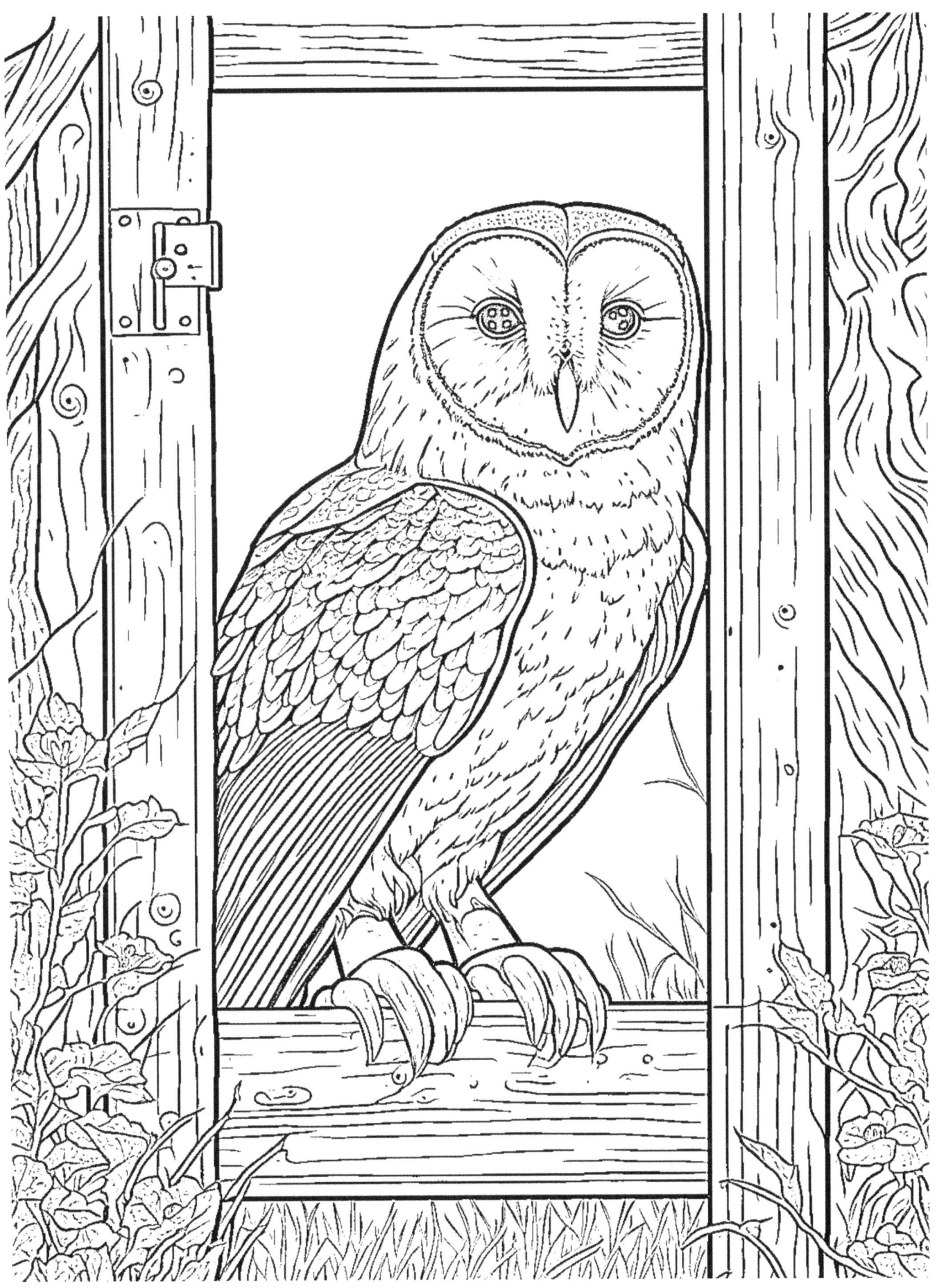

12 - Barn Owl

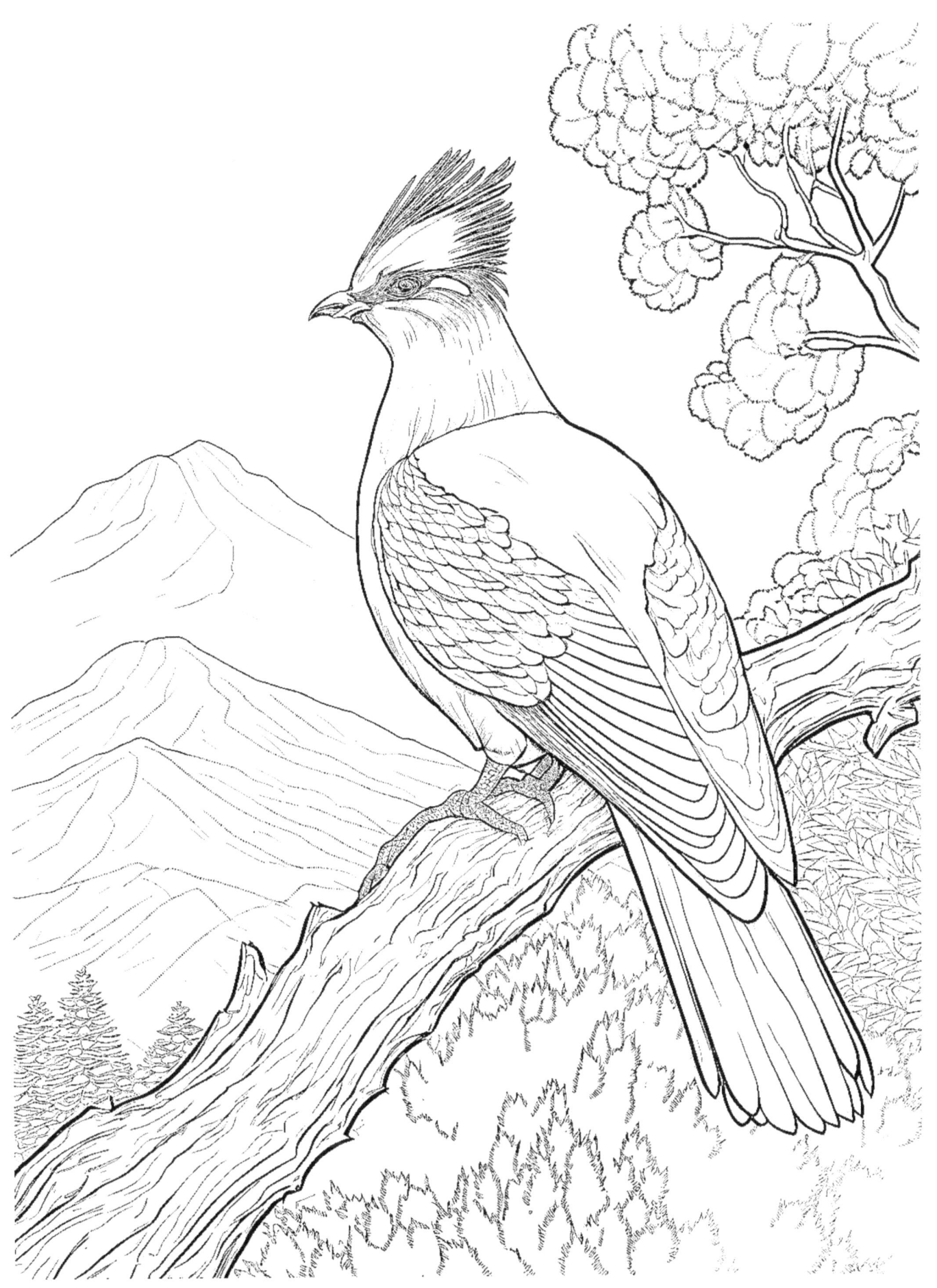

13 - Blue Crowned Pigeon

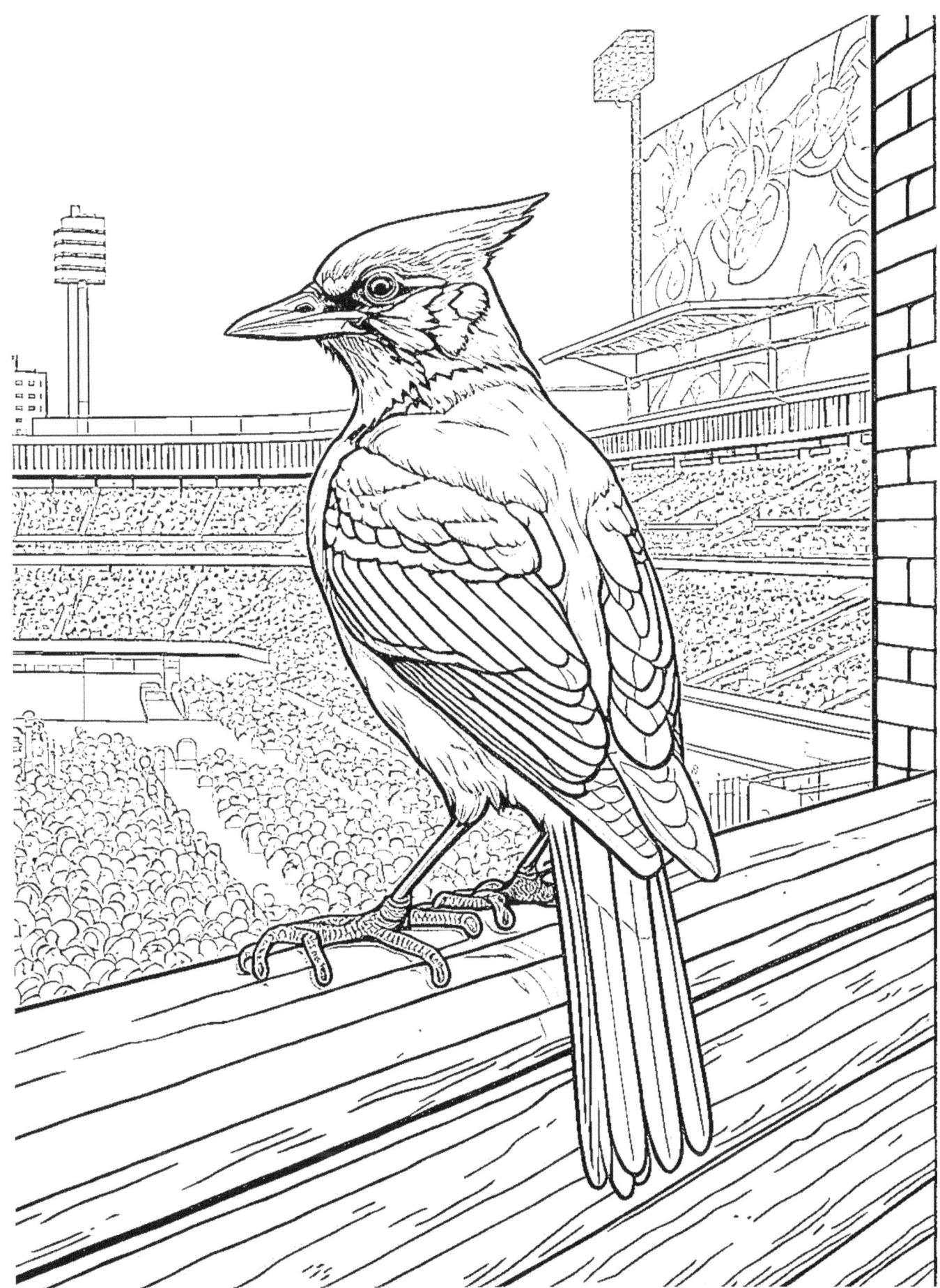

14 - Blue Jay

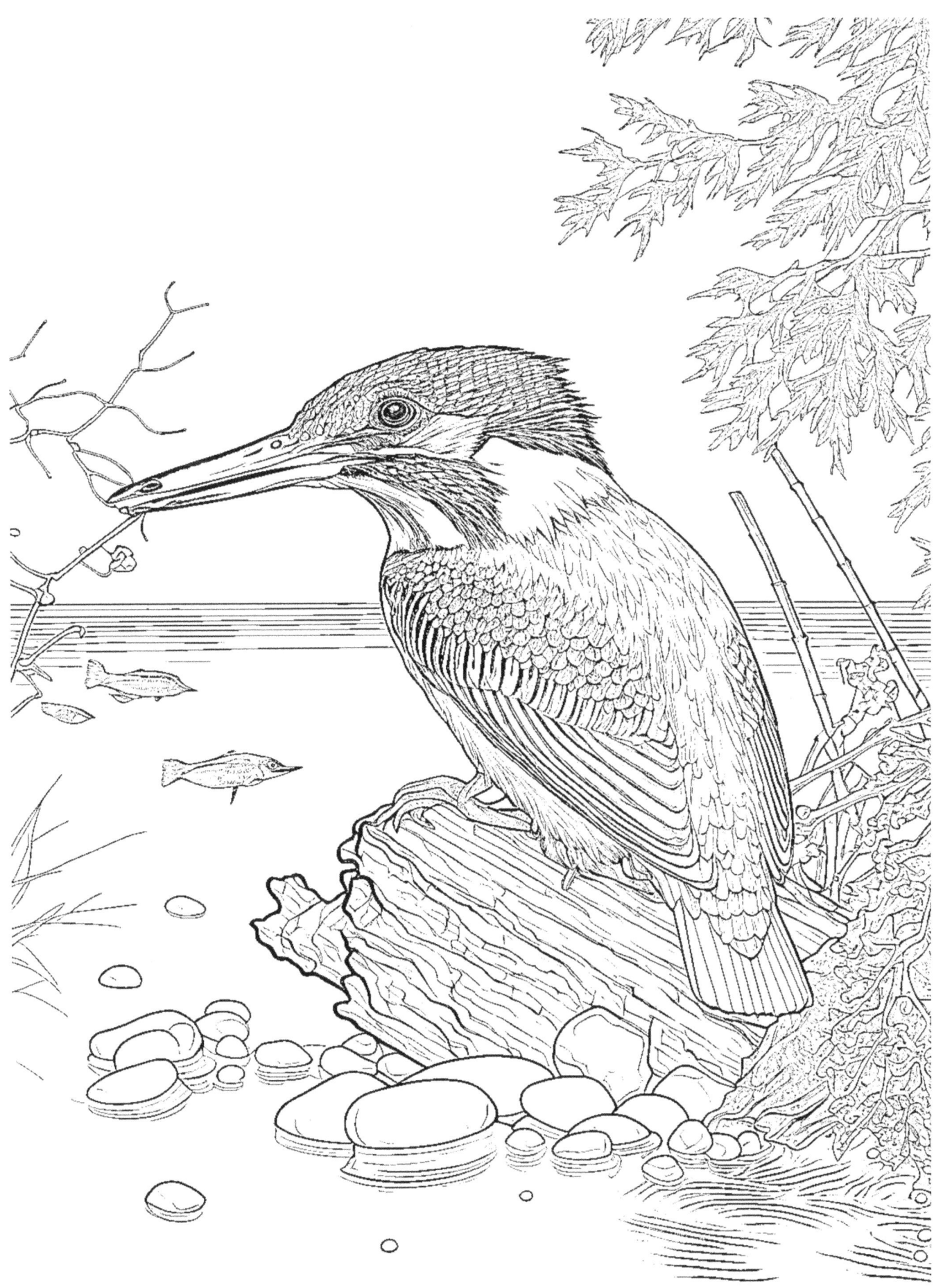

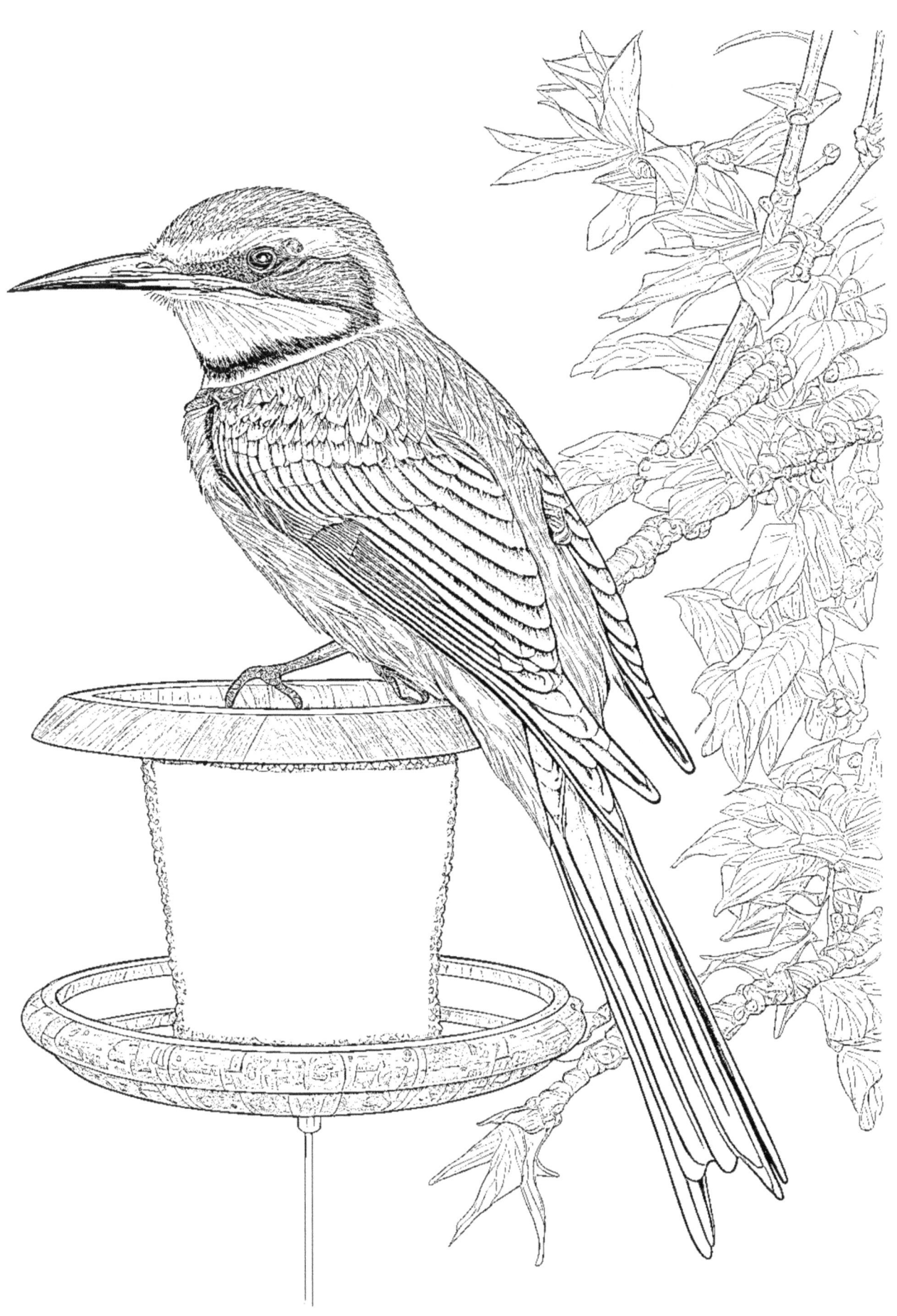

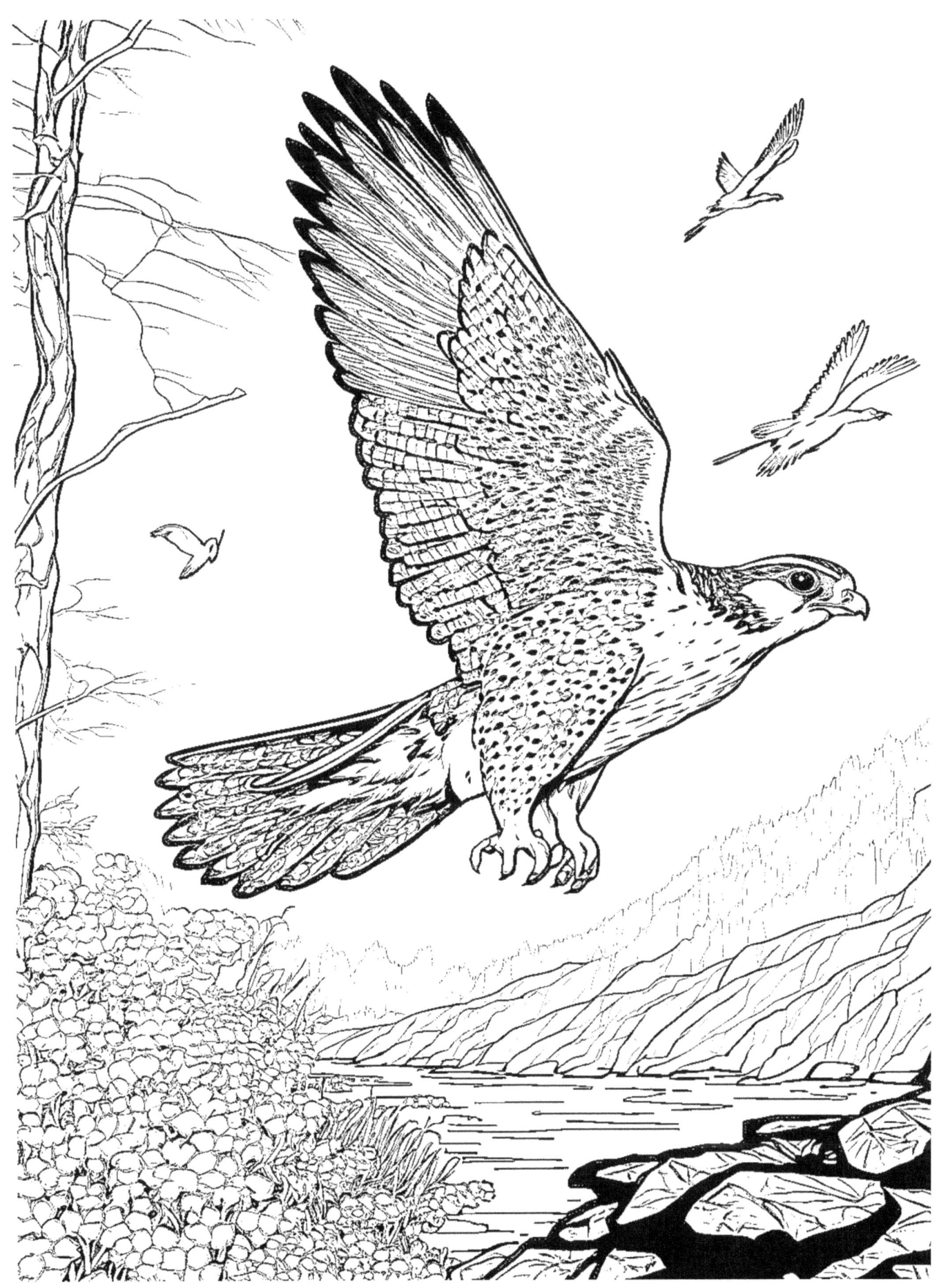

17 - Falcon

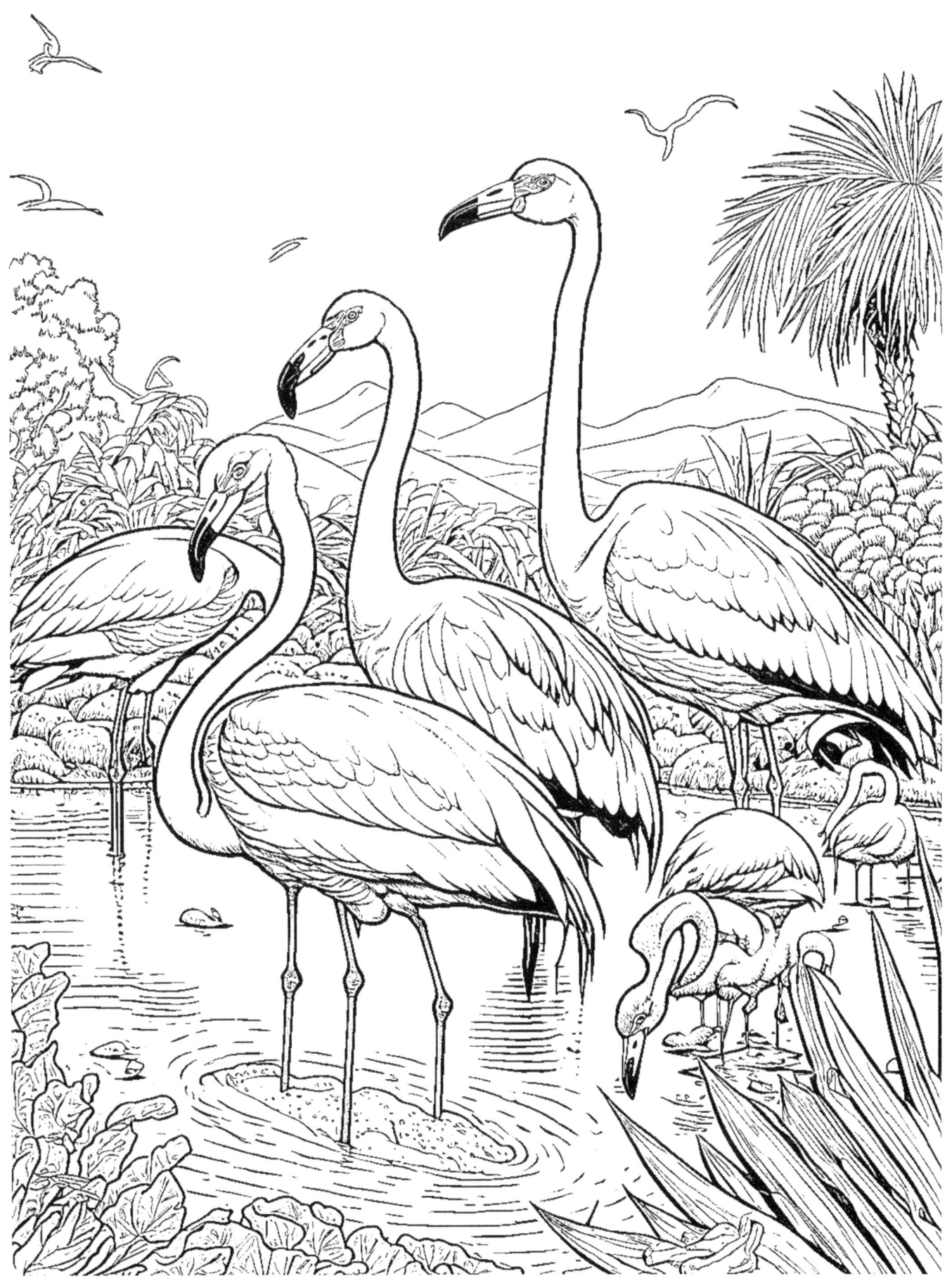

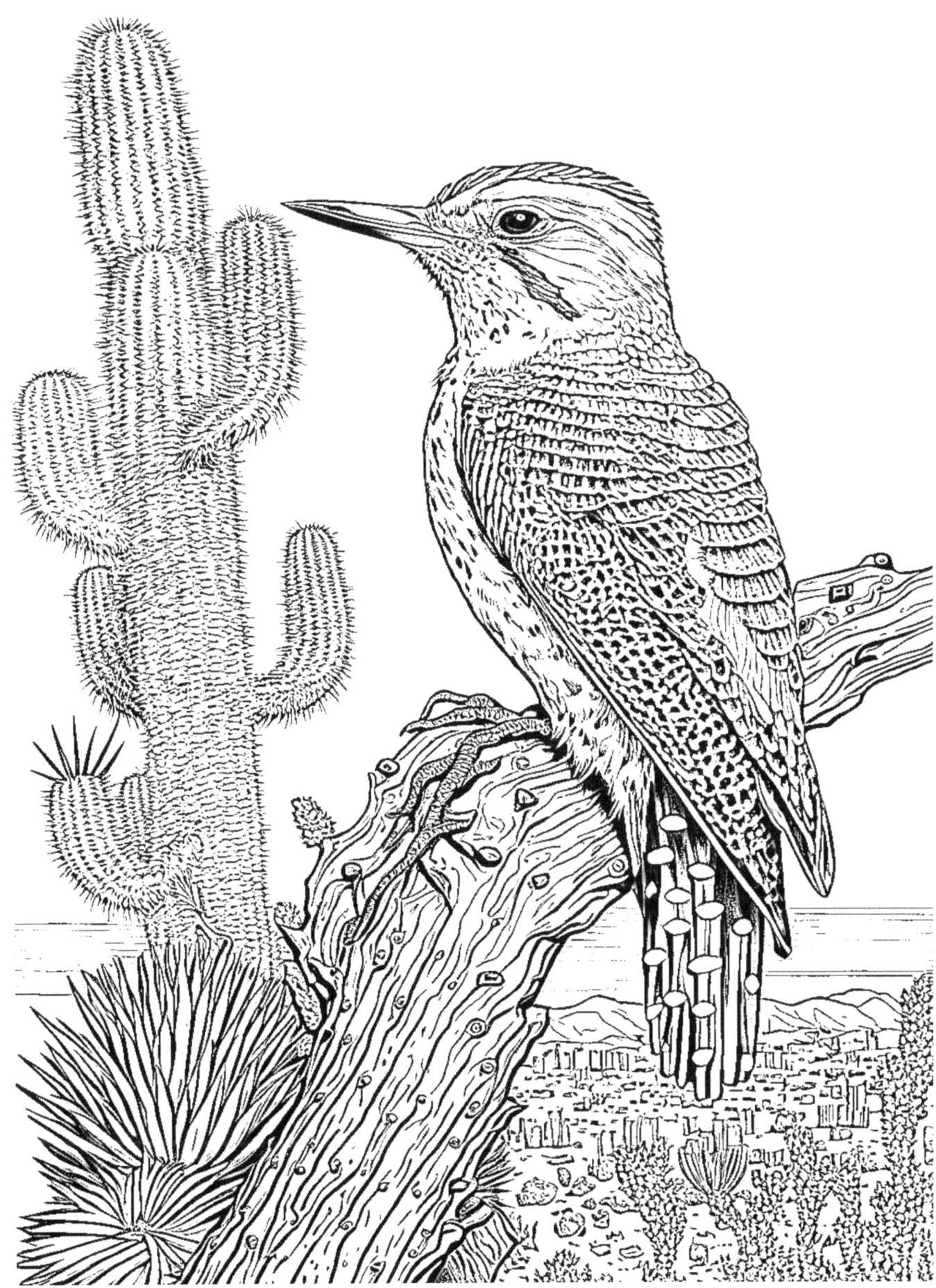

19 - Gila Woodpecker

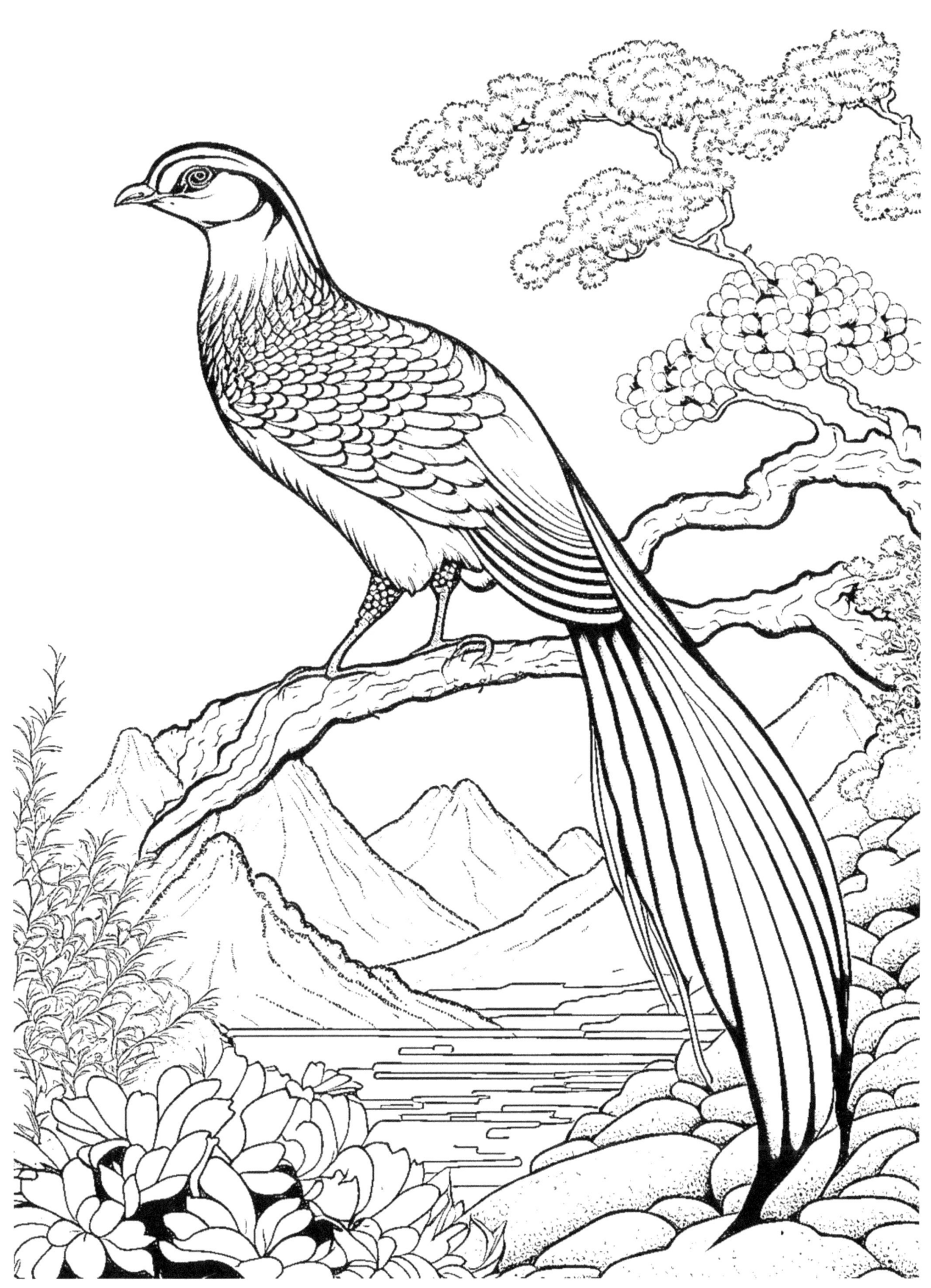

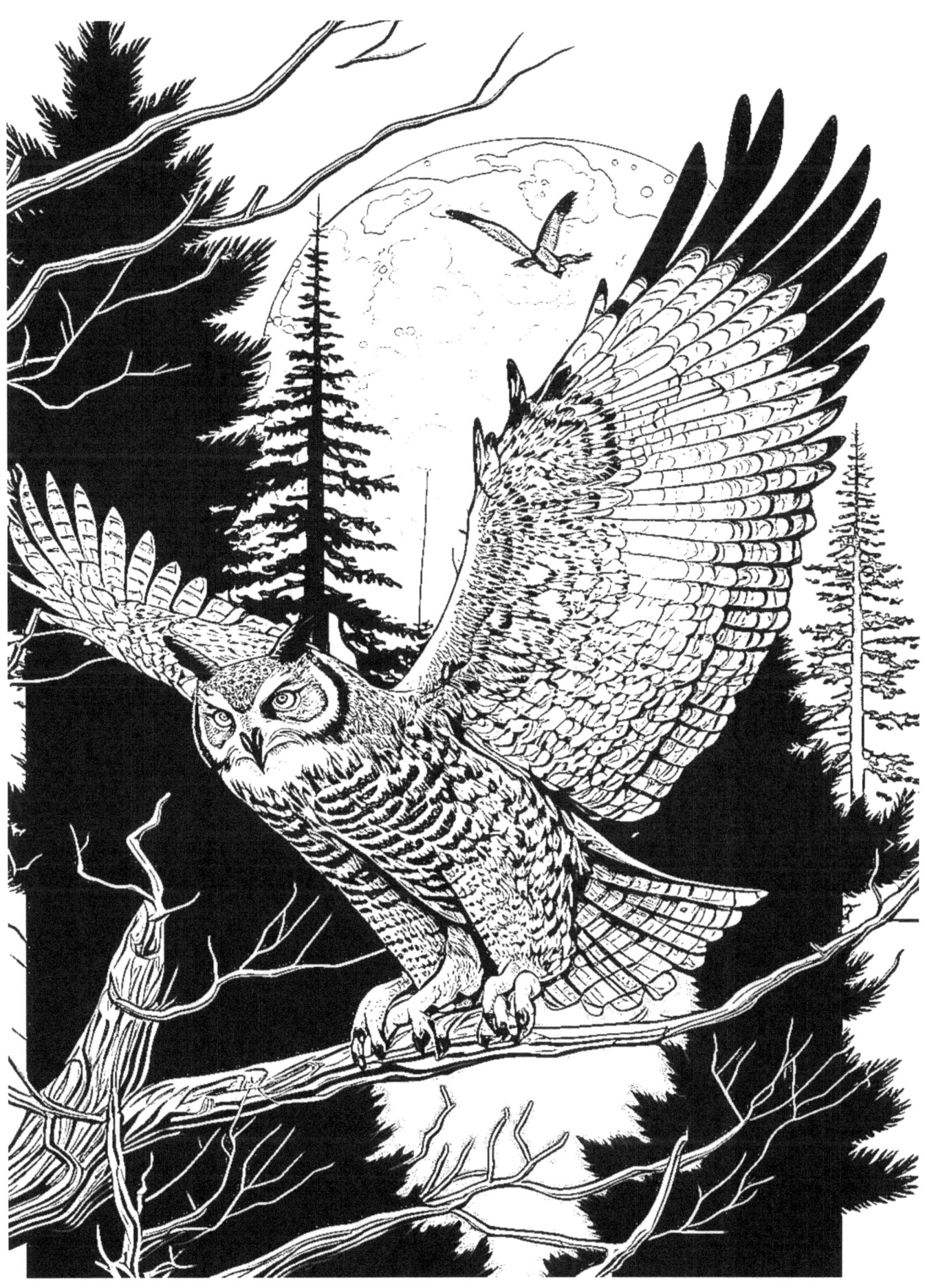

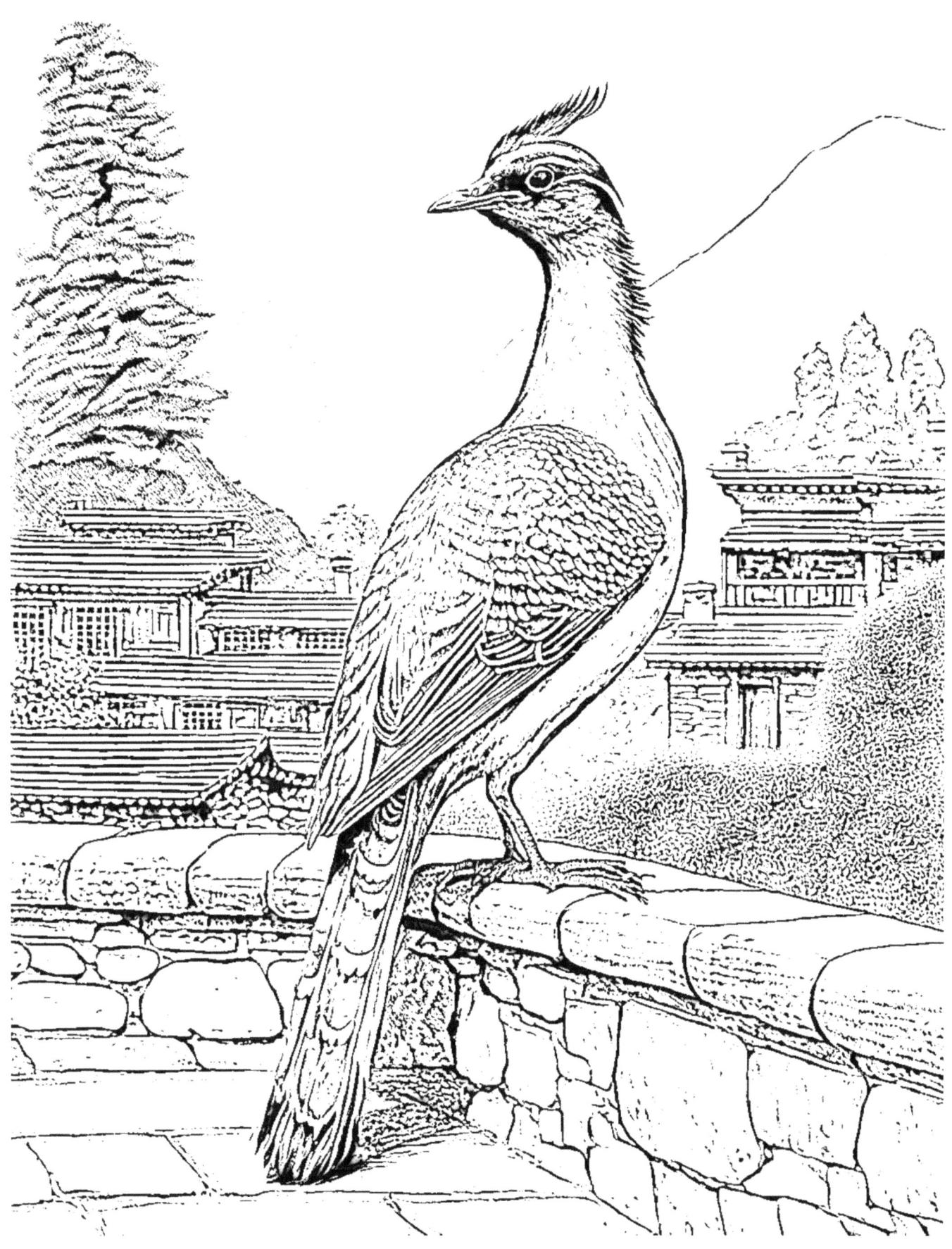

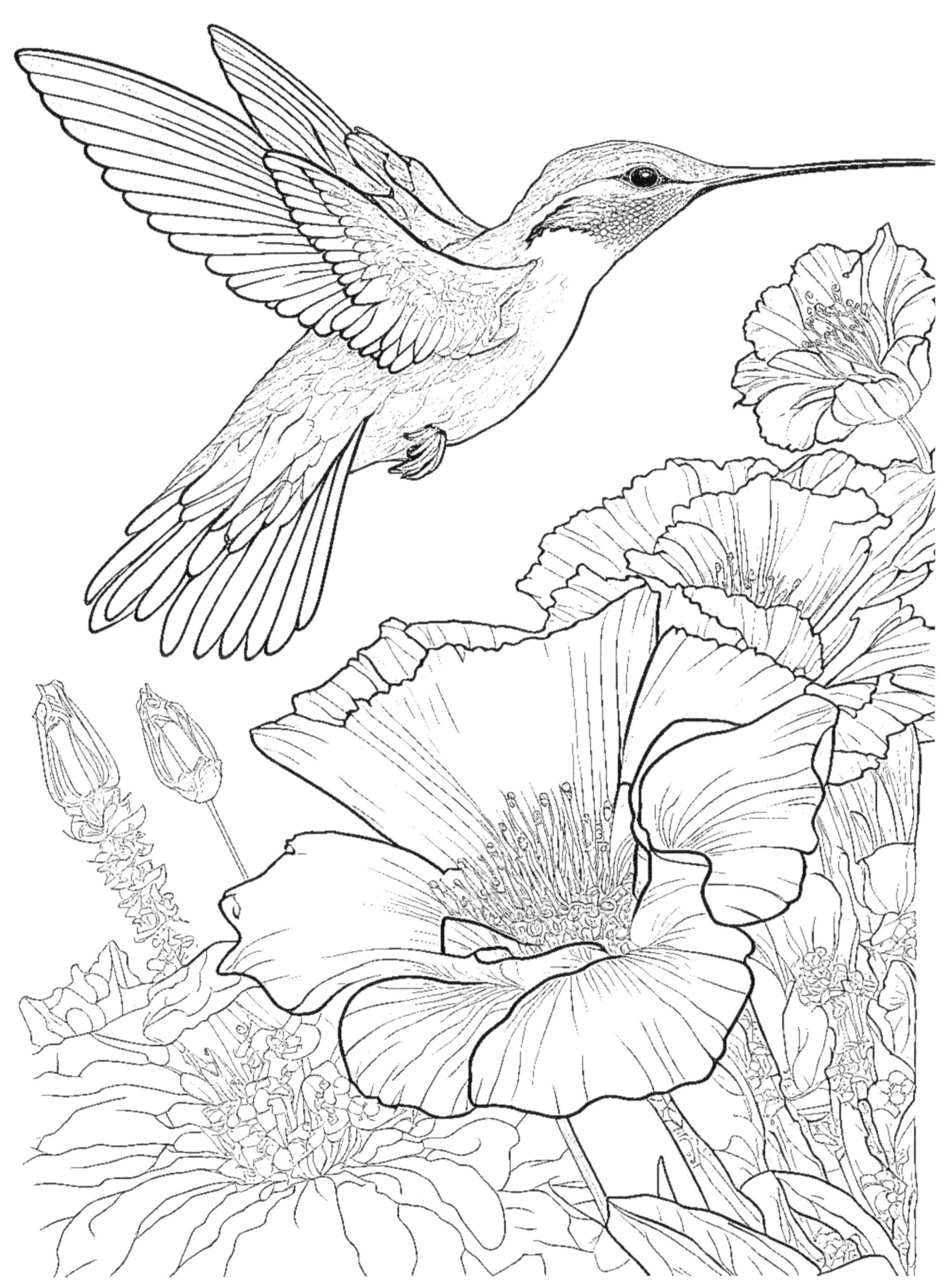

23 - Hummingbird

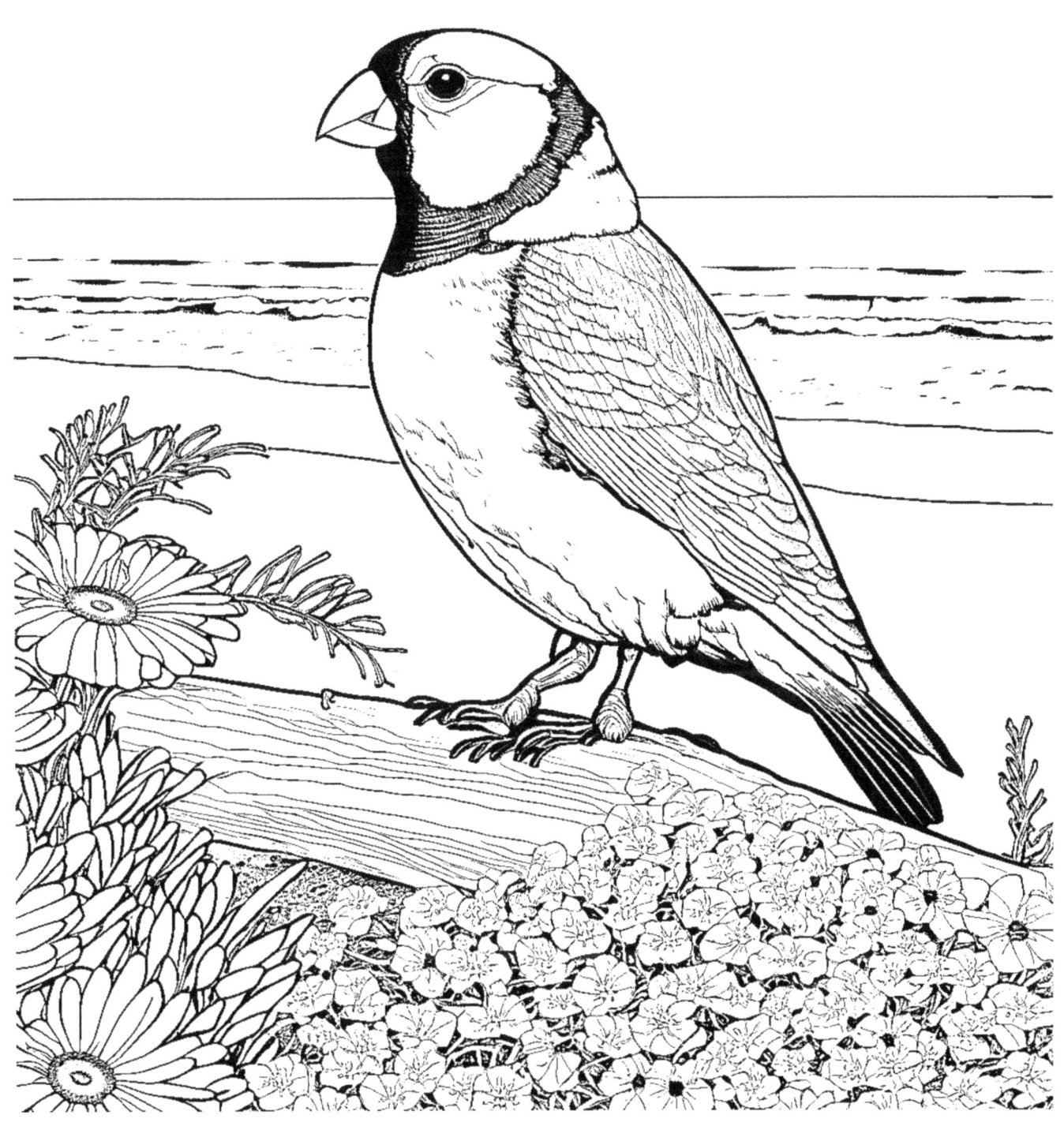

24 - Lady Gouldian Finch

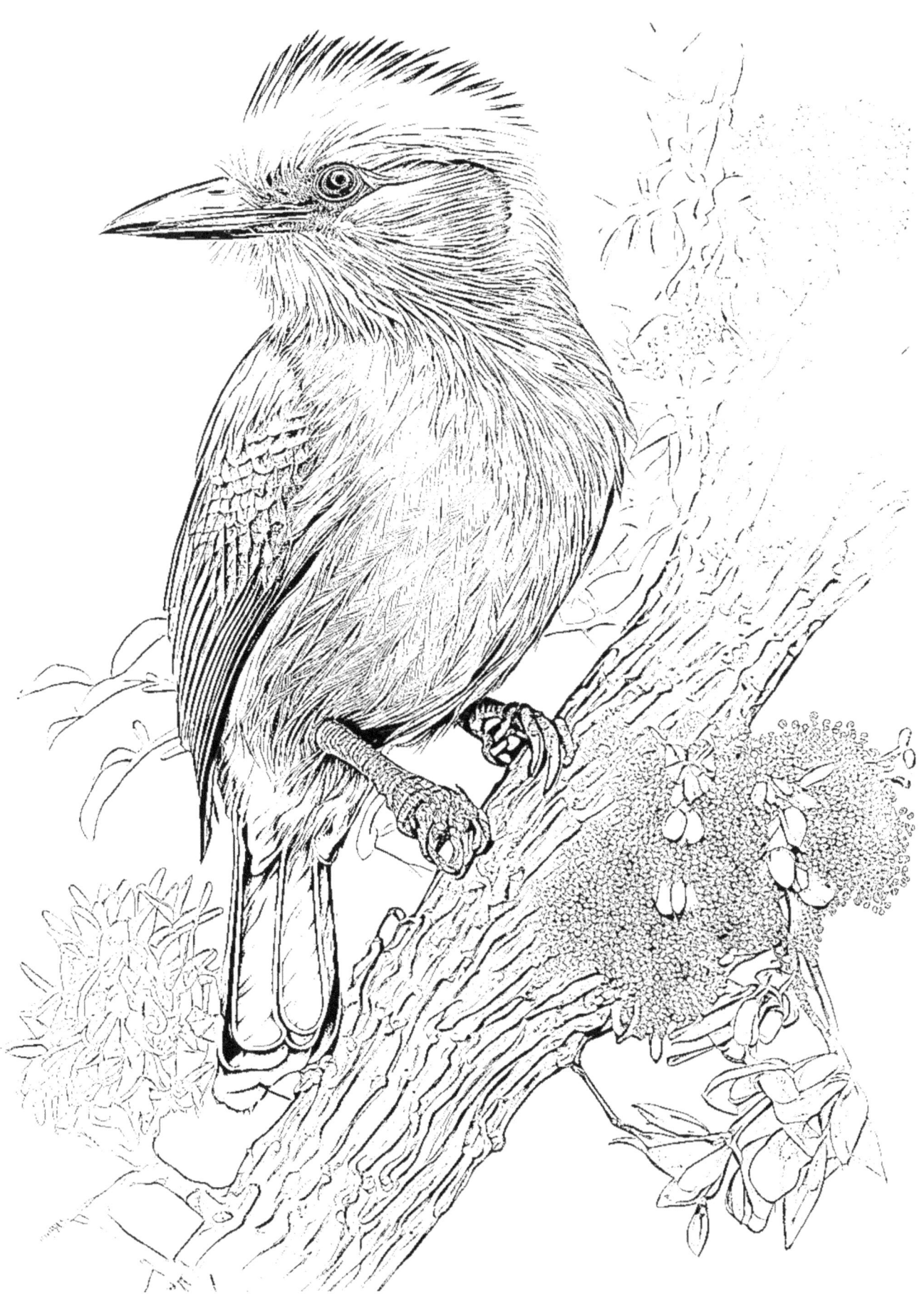

25 - Lilac Crested Roller

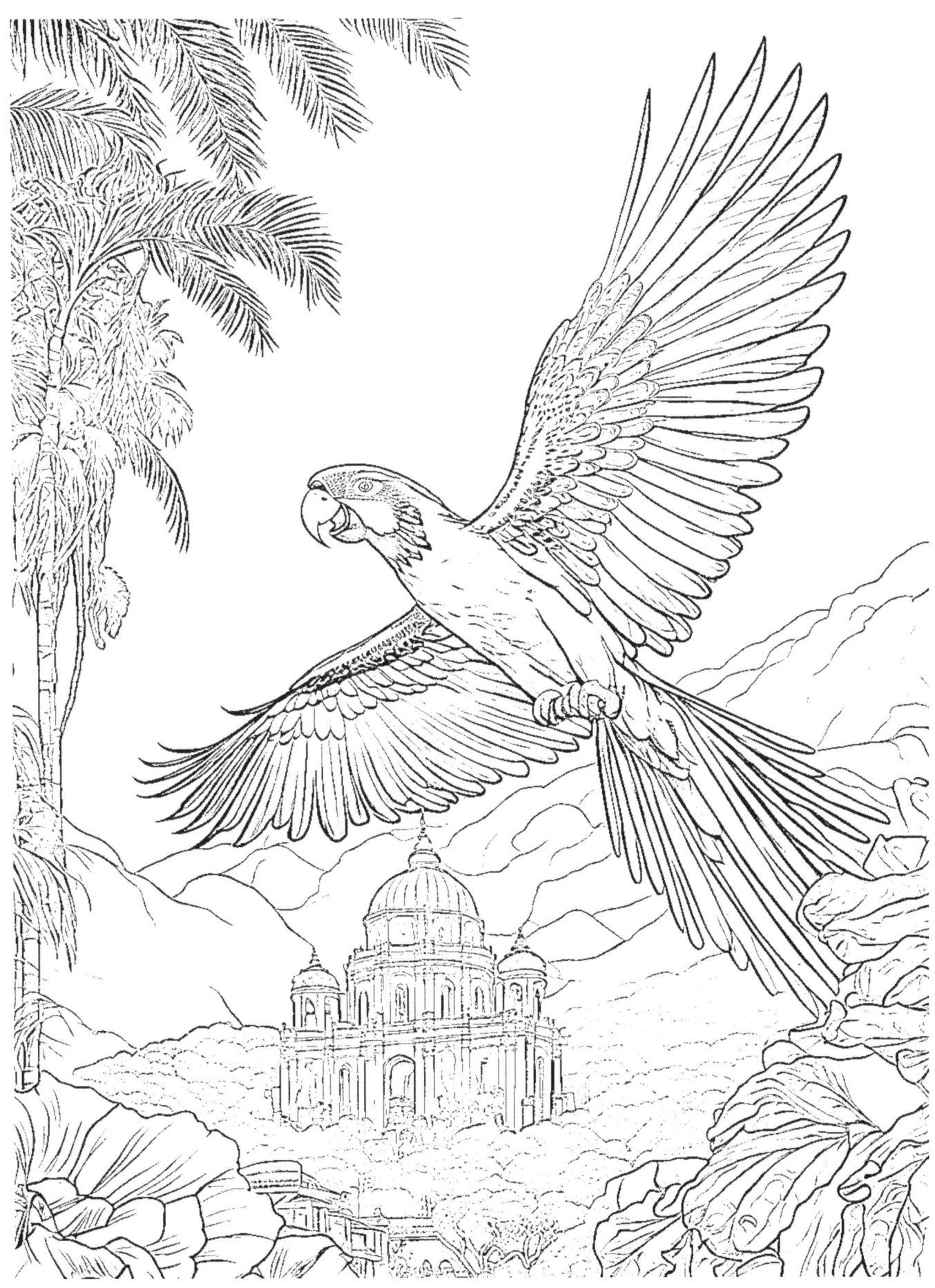

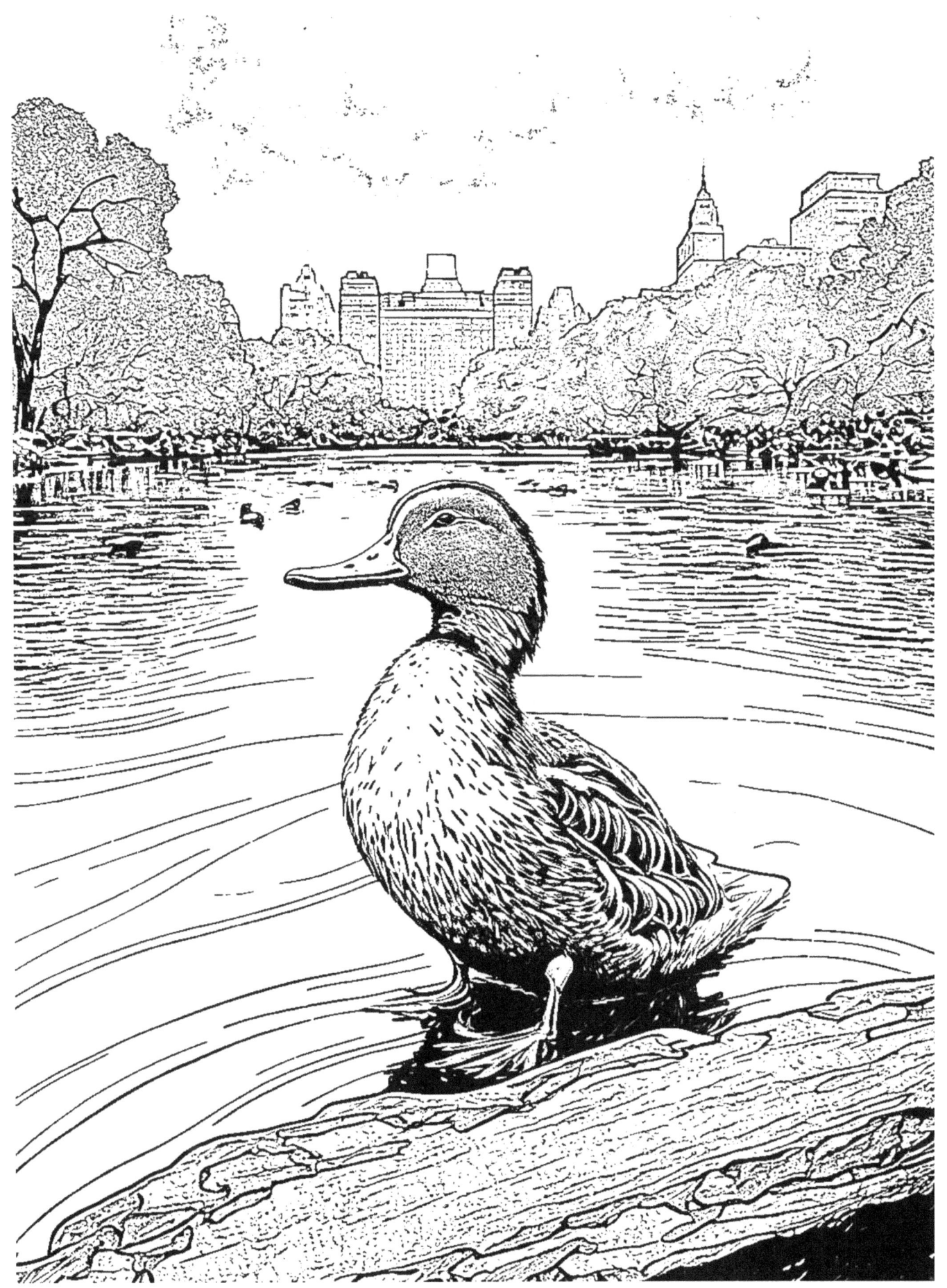

27 - Mallard

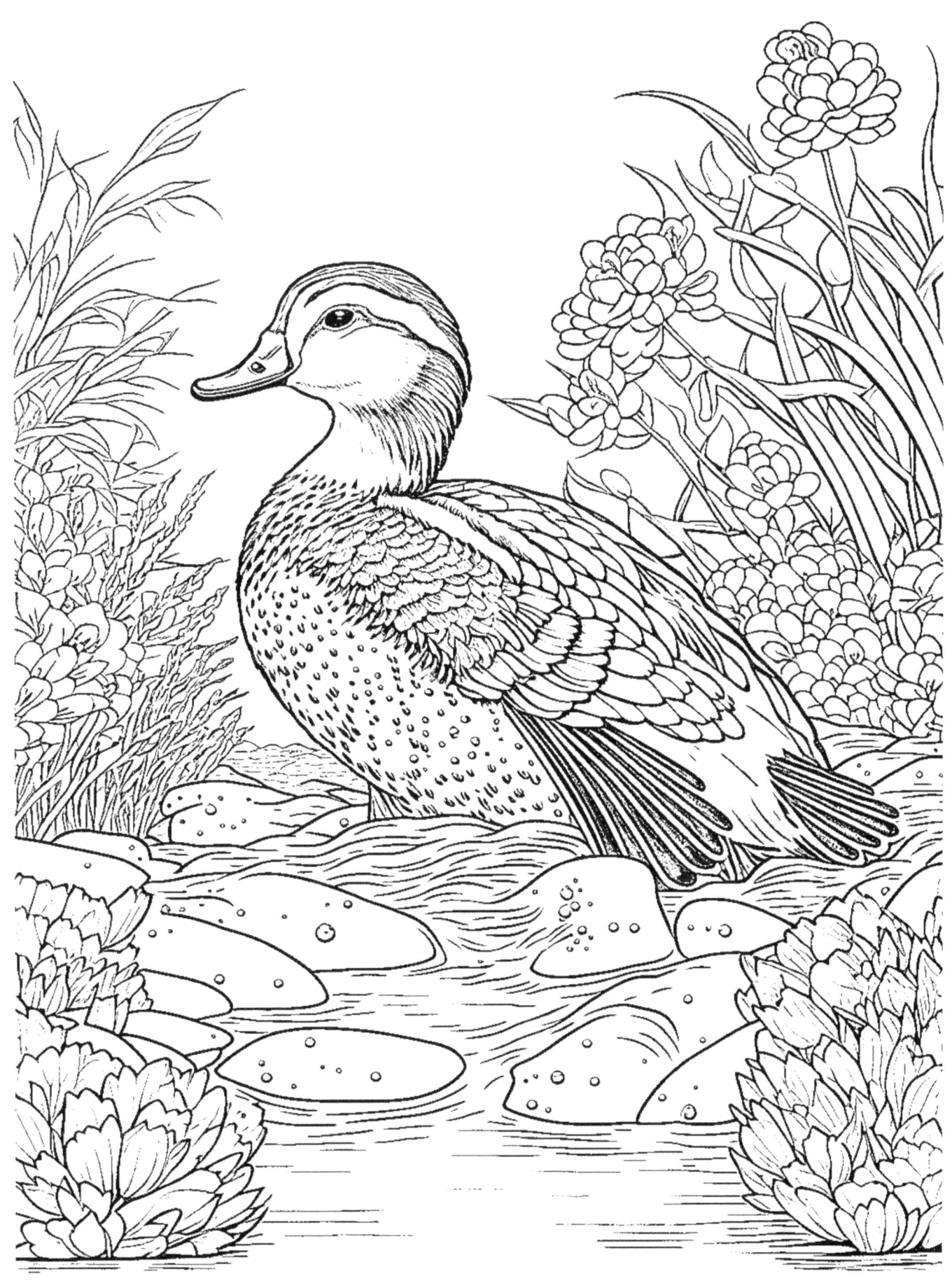

28 - Mandarin Duck

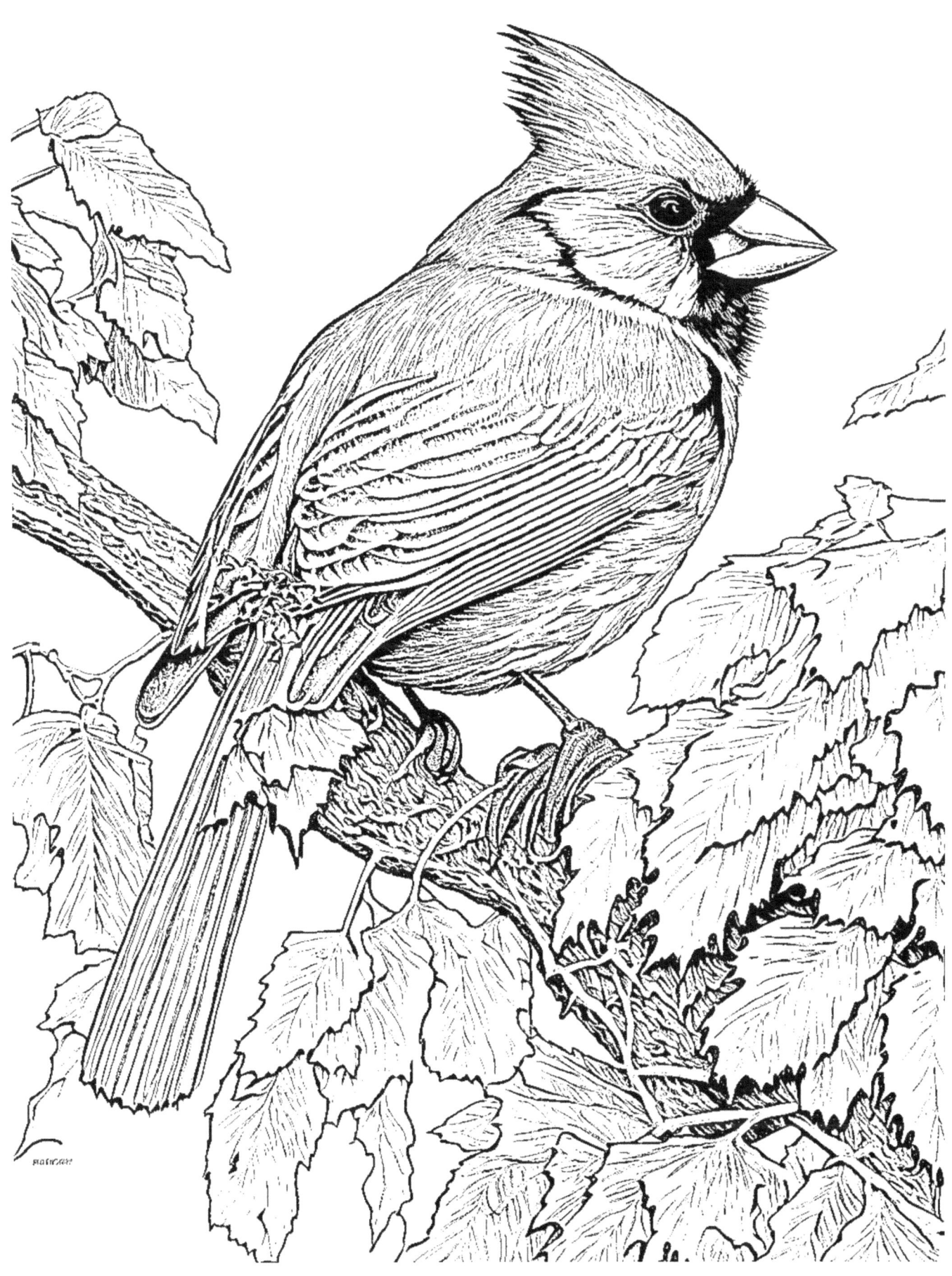

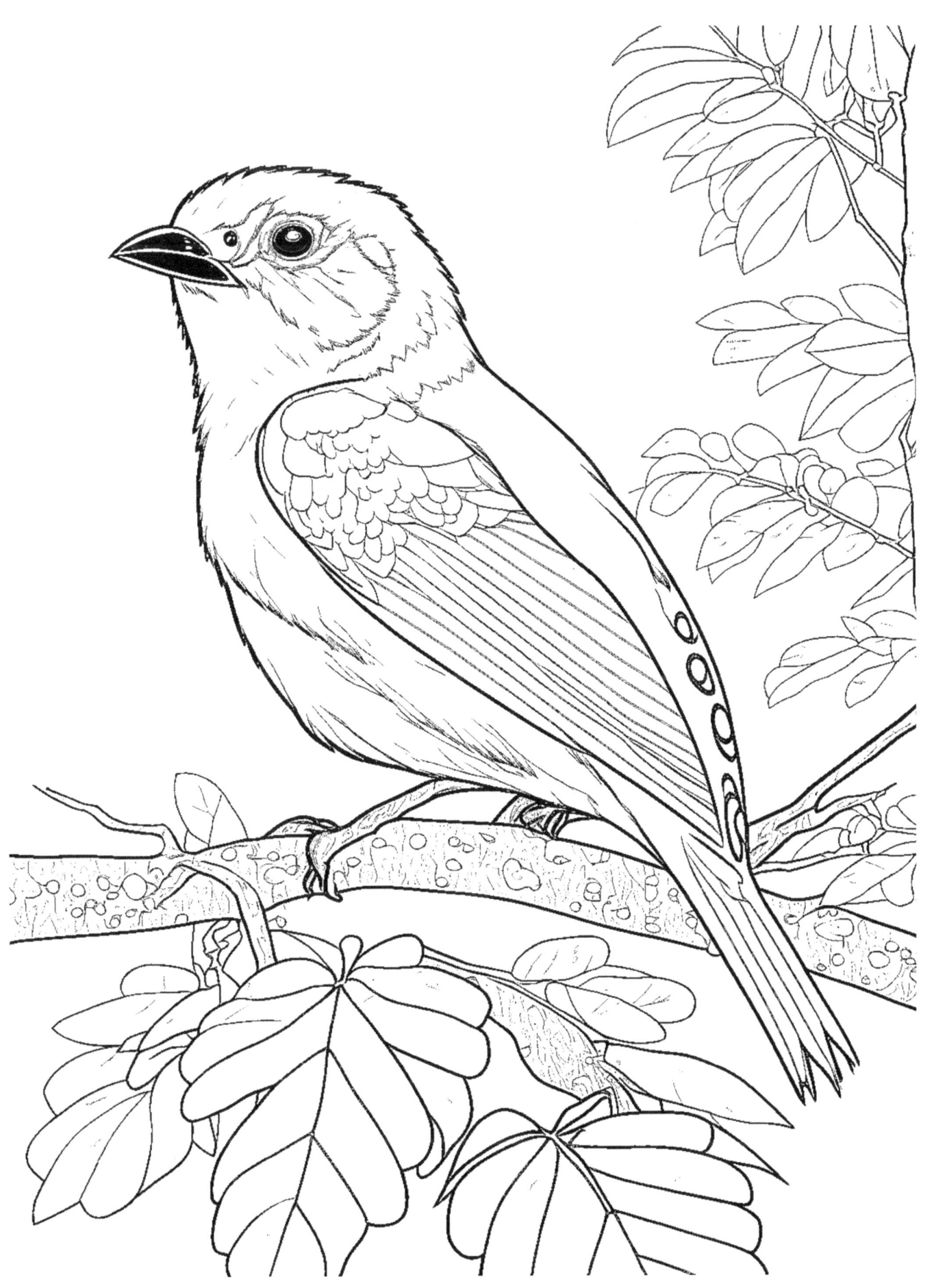

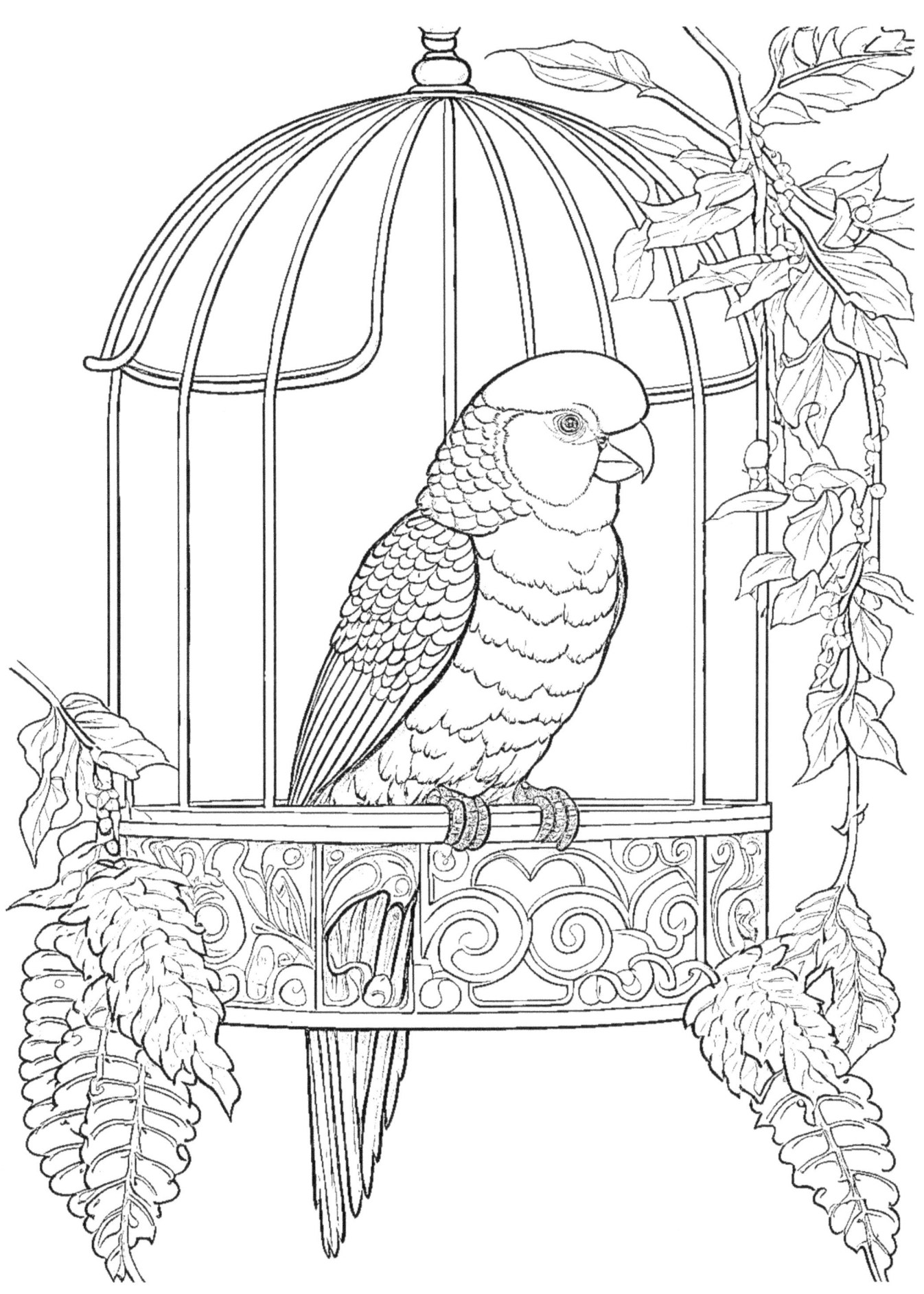

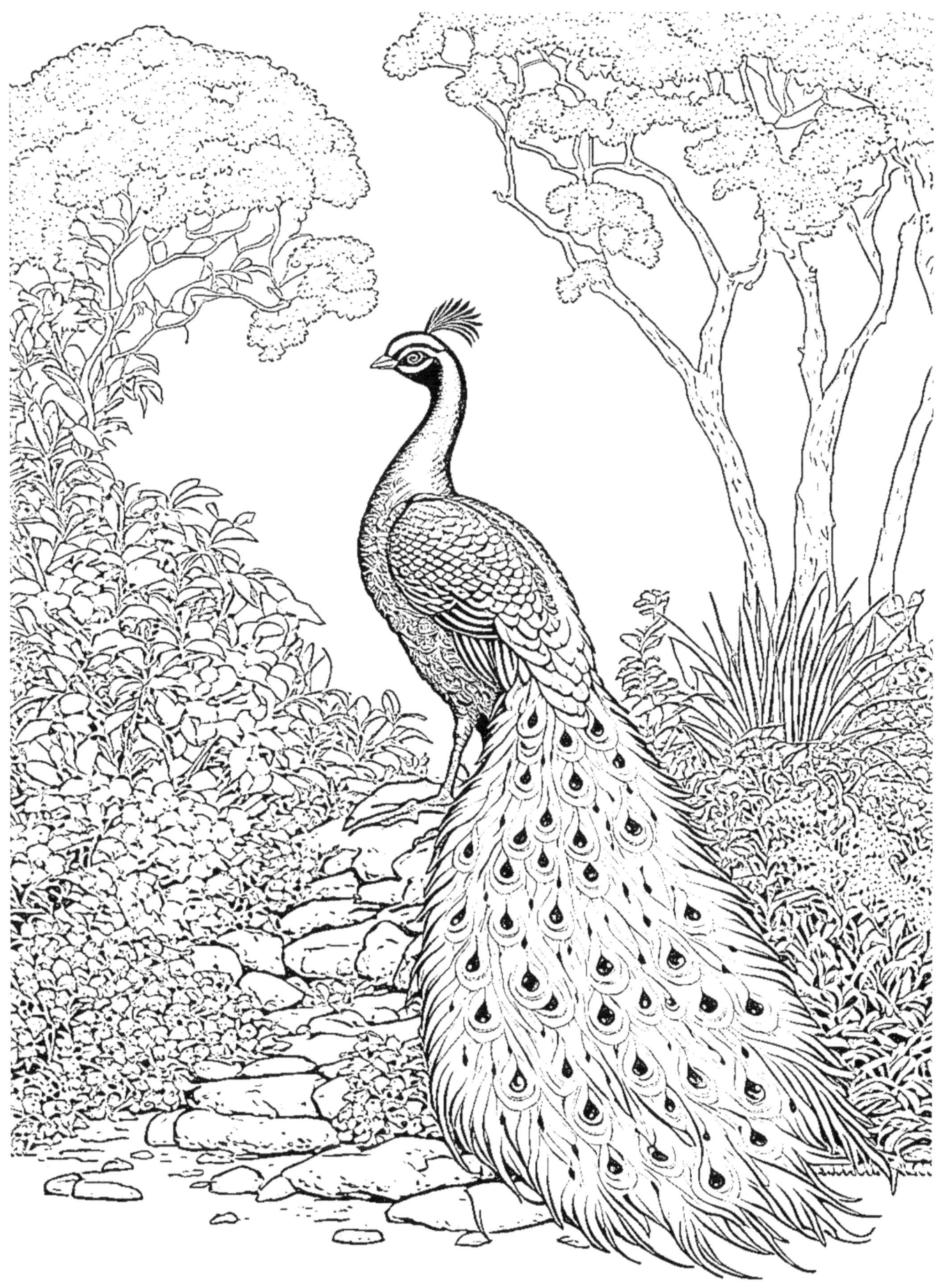

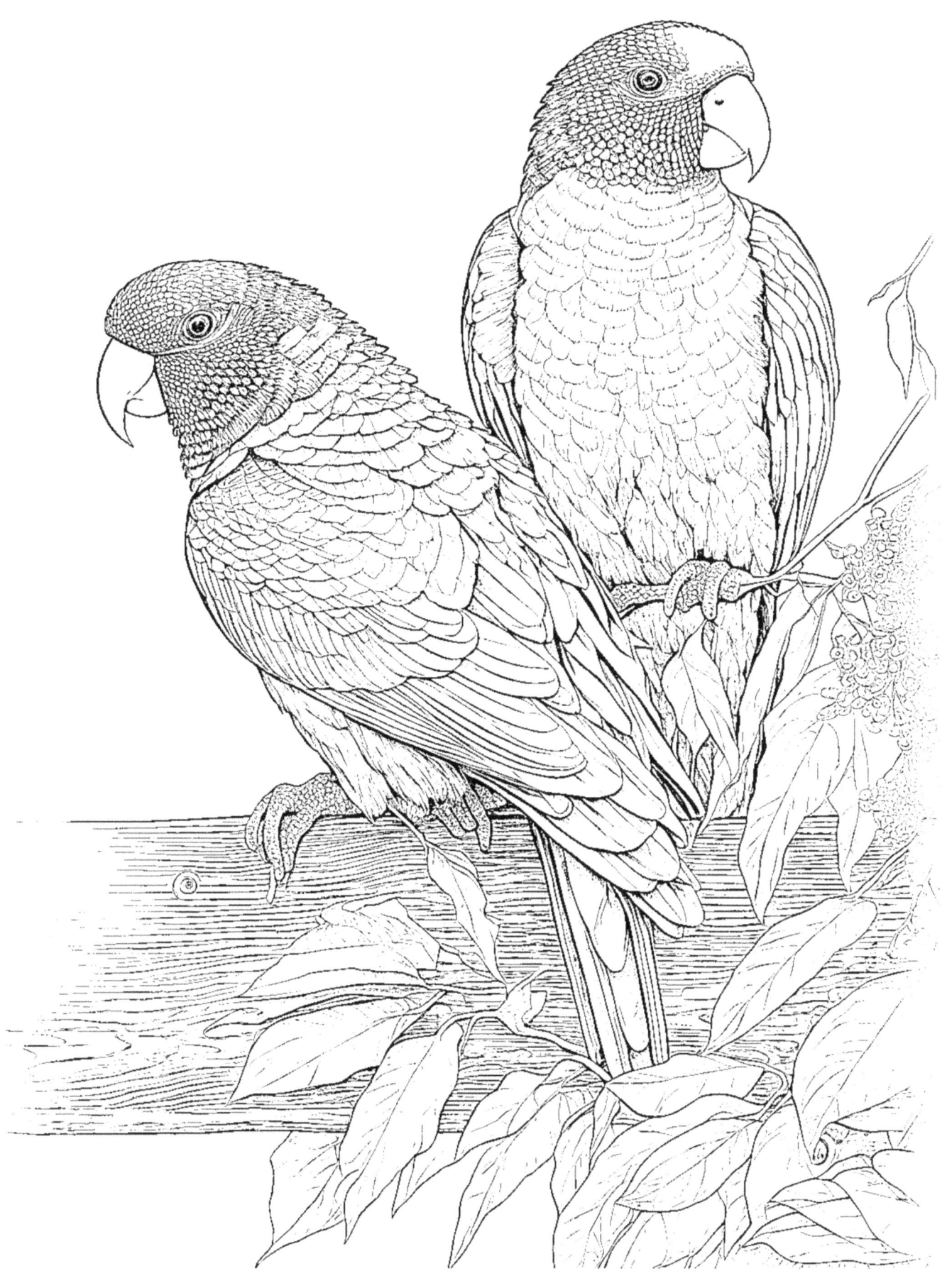

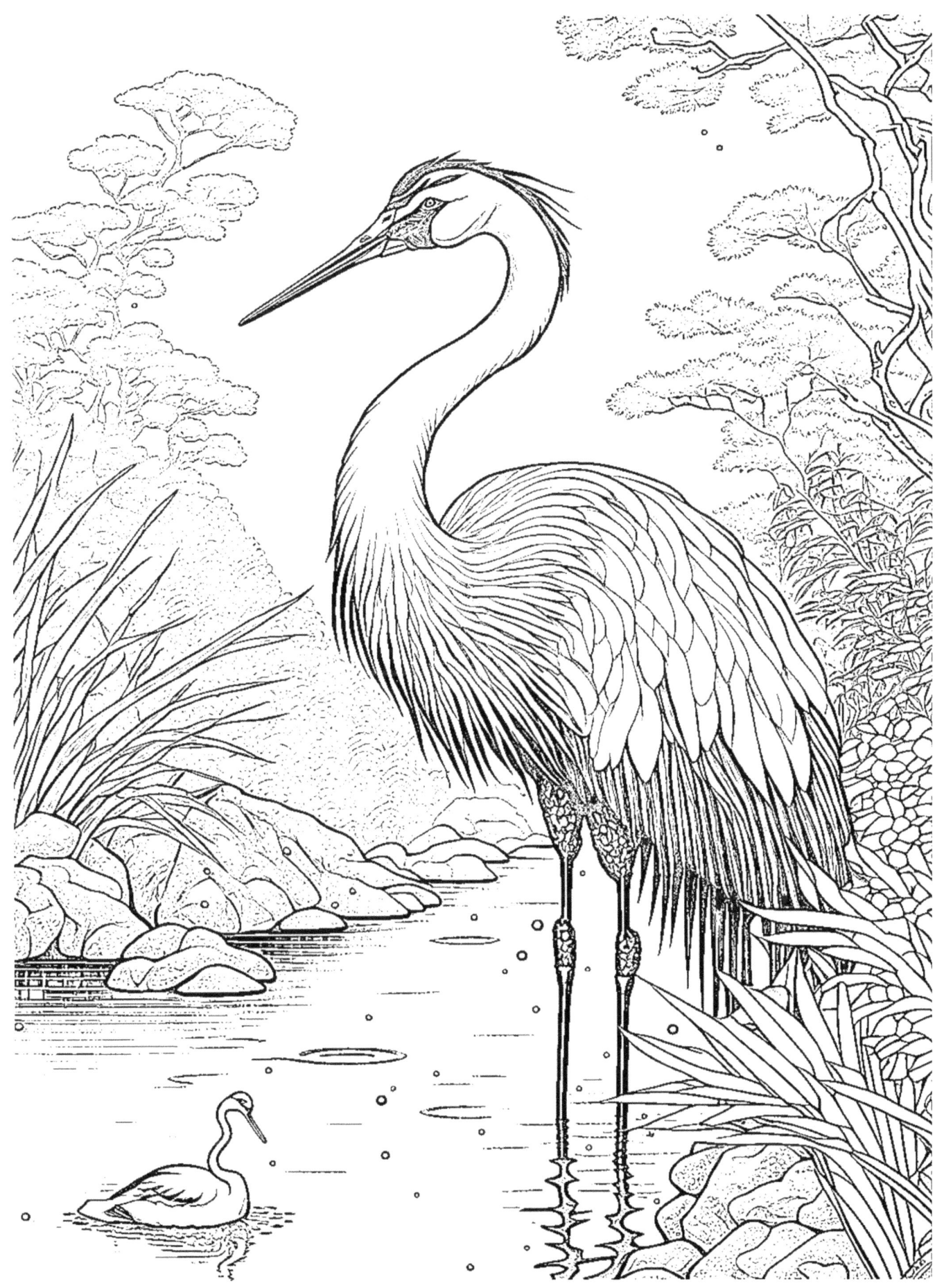

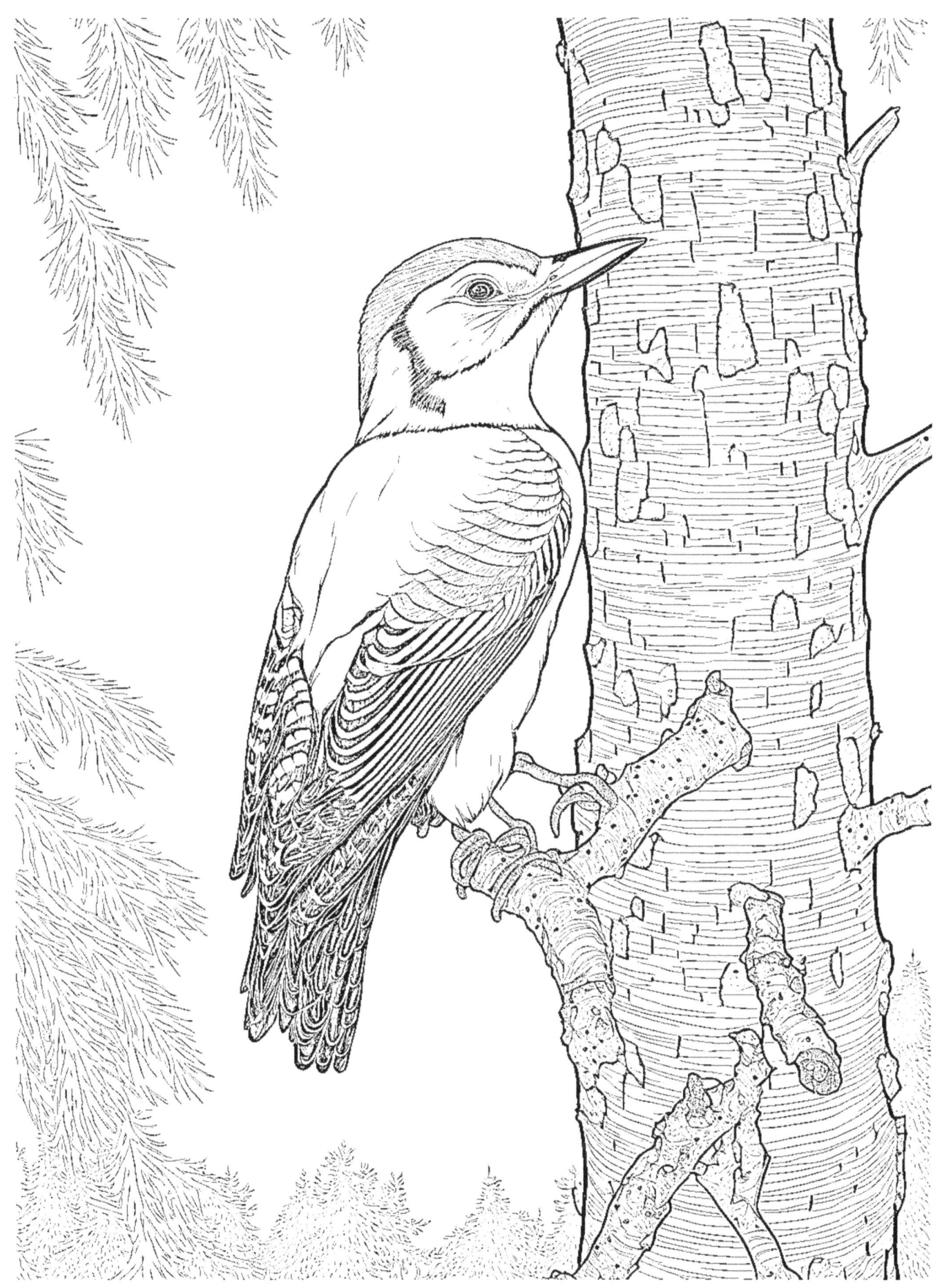

35 - Red Headed Woodpecker

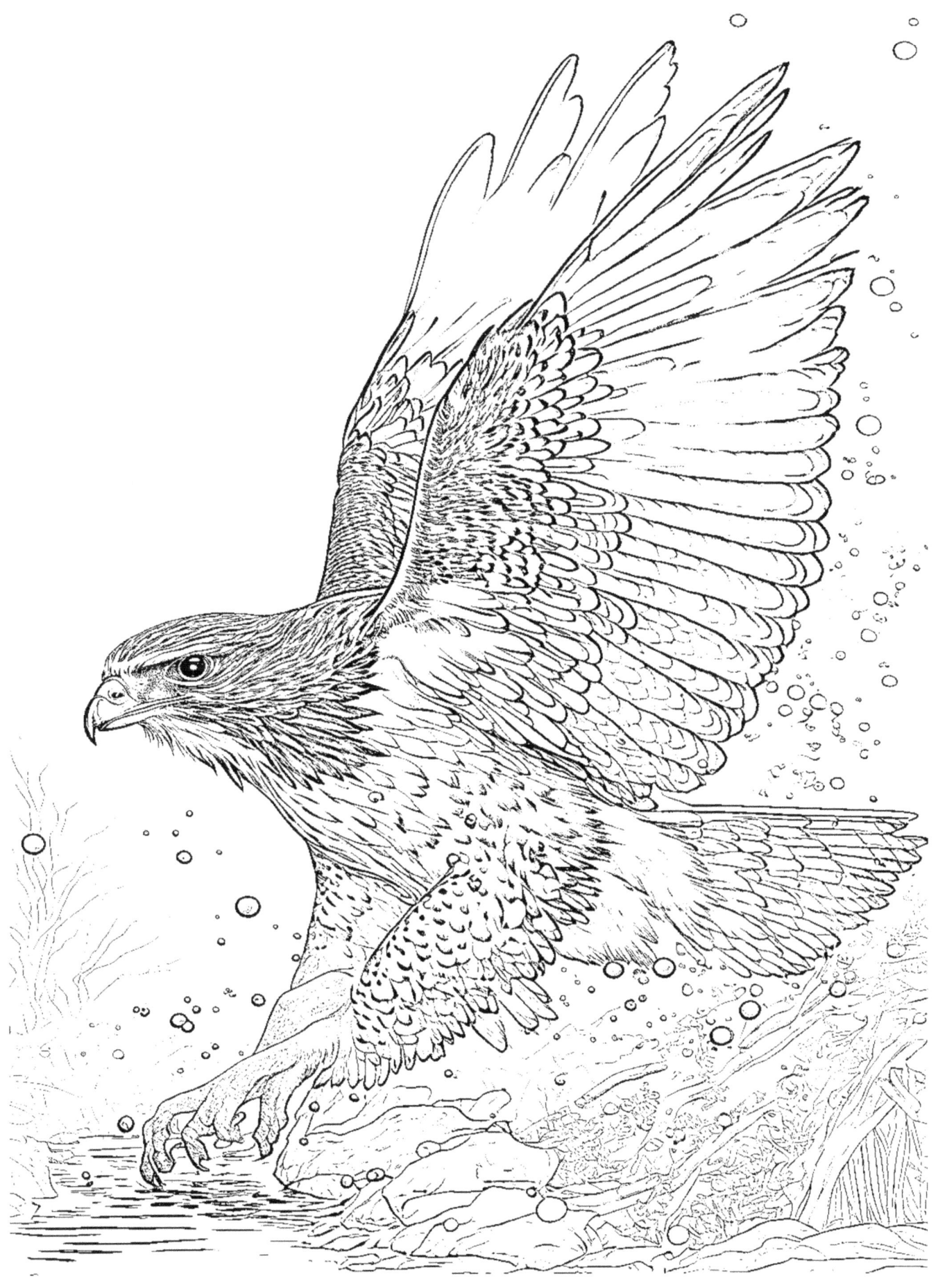

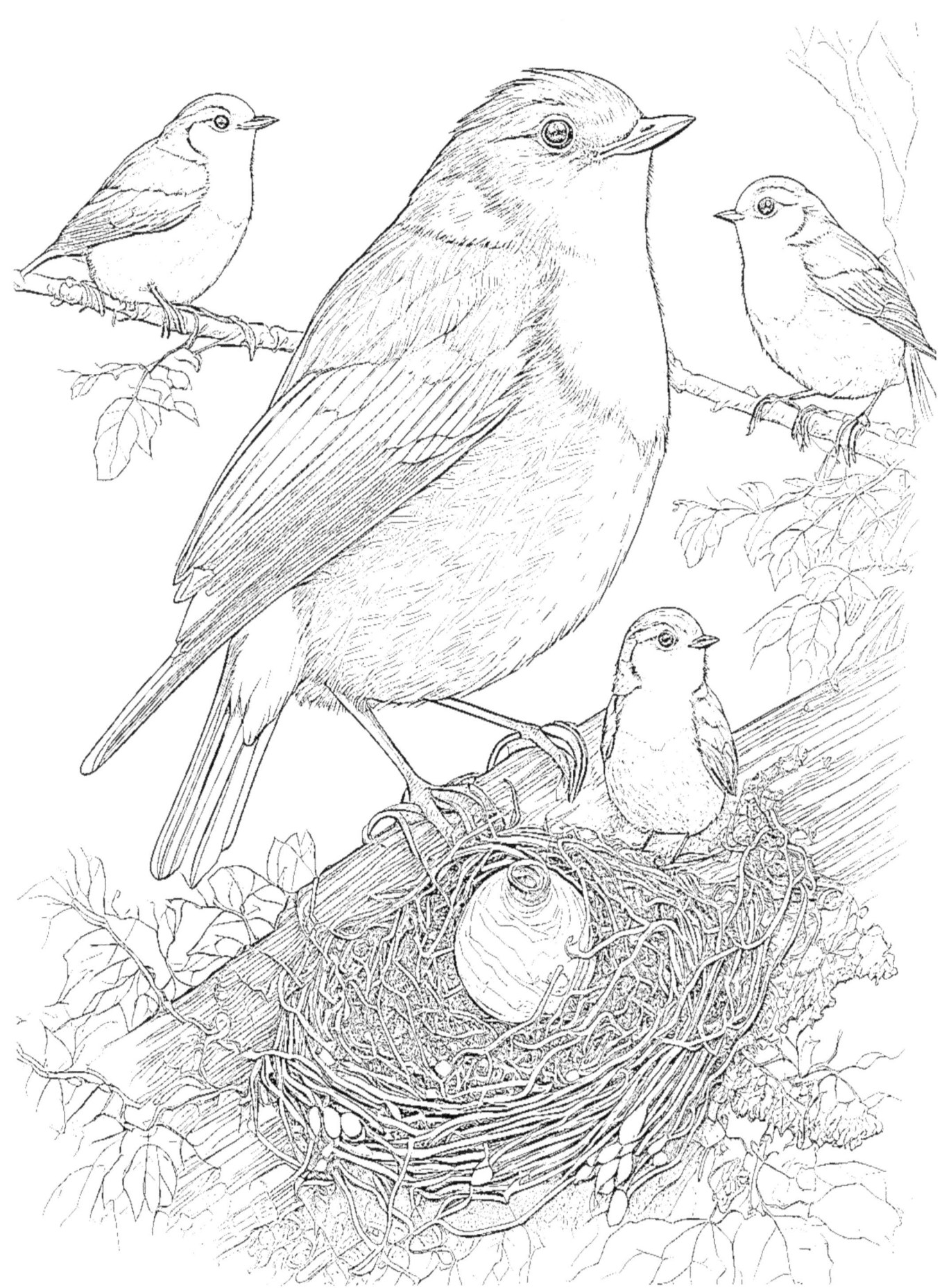

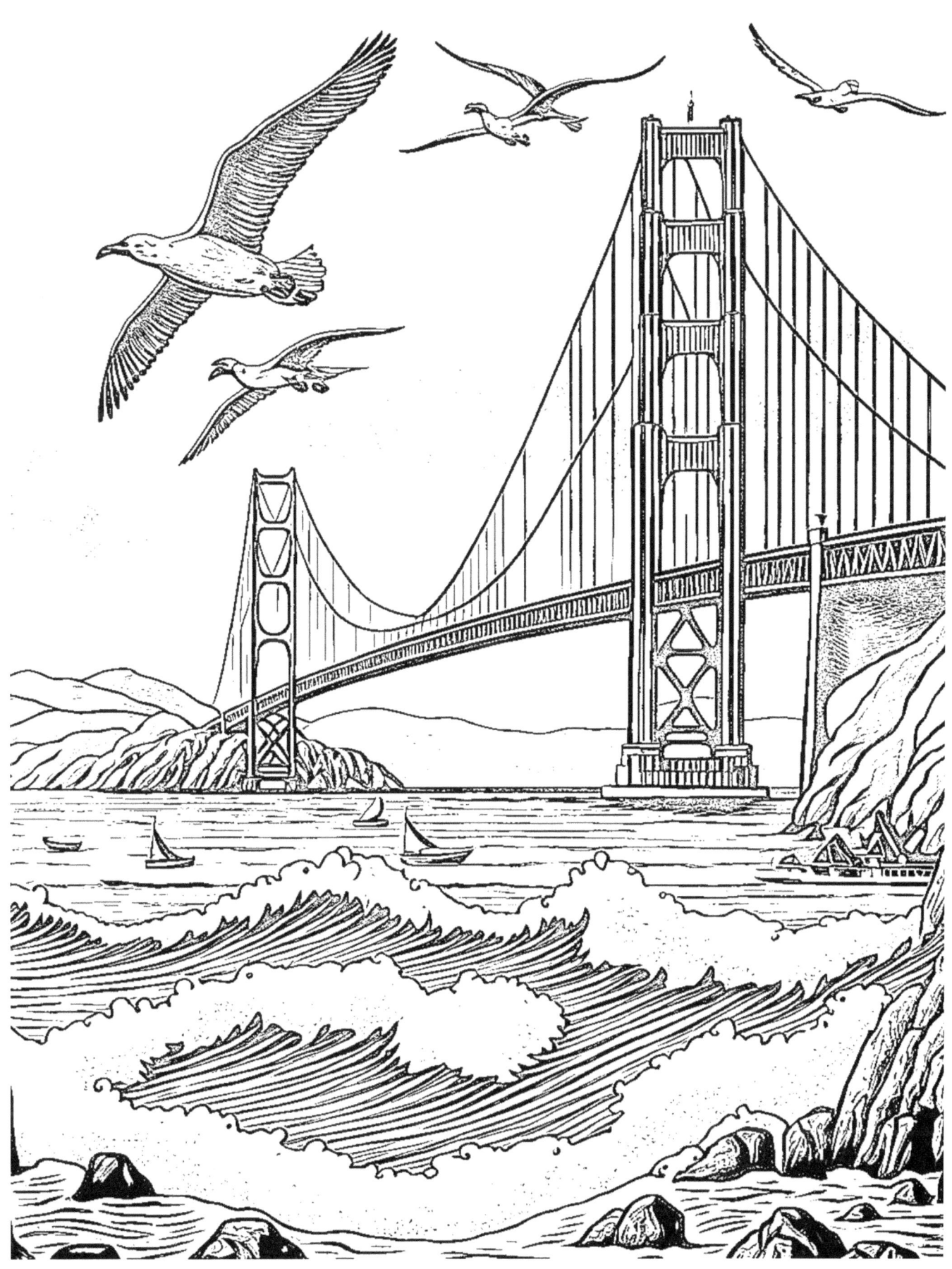

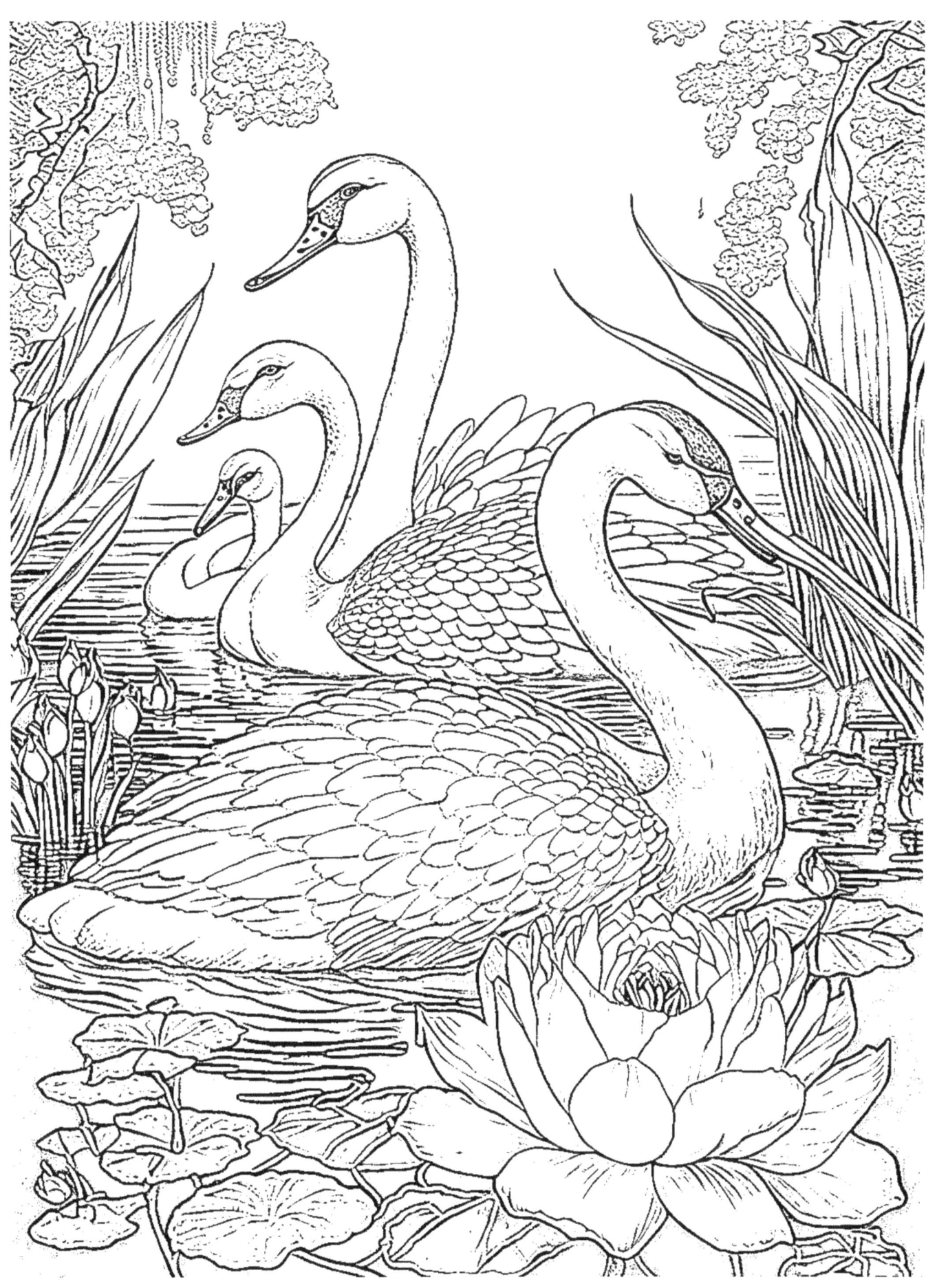

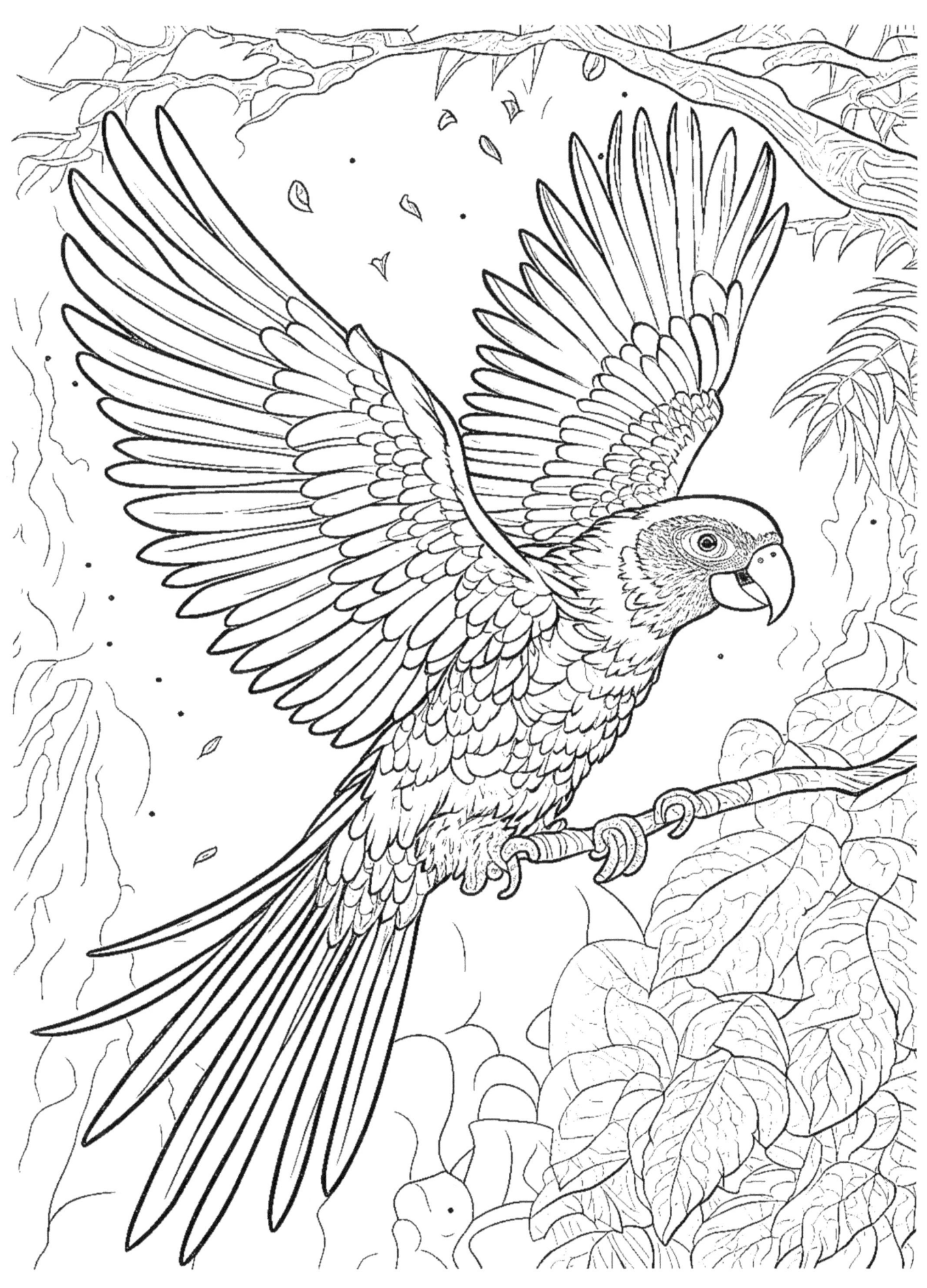